The words that took us there

Just a girl

There was a girl
I used to be
With no sense of direction
She had the words to take me there

I was a girl
She used to be
In a life of beginnings
I only caught the endings

There was a girl
She did not weep
She did not cry
And I mourned for her

She was the girl
I tried to be
Little we spoke
Just the words that took us there

Eveline Edz, *Just a girl*

Table of Contents

Acknowledgements

This is for Pau, who chose to stay and whom I love beyond words.

I would like to thank the following people for helping me in some big or small way:

Julie (impressed with the prose you gave me while role-playing), David (wish distance wasn't such a limiting factor, love ya), Irene (you spend your last 20 bucks on a phone call, how can I forget; thanks for everything), Karen (where have you gone?), Andrea (Amsterdam's a nice port of call you know), Steve (I don't think "terse" is in your vocabulary), Paul (thanks for the original artwork), Richard (for being patient and teaching me the very, very basics).

Arrienne (loved fighting with you), Merlin (*lick!*), mr. simon (with respect), Maia (I won't forget the wonderful hours in your sunlit apartment), Kannika (we've been through a lot), Alaria (never did talk with you enough), Datafluxx (you were so cool!), Tôsama (yes, I changed your name throughout as you wanted; thanks for everything and more, you know who you are), Inquisitor (the legend... thanks for talking), A.C. (damn you were annoying, and that's a compliment *grin*), Annique (glad you liked my home made 'fashion'), Bill Door (for talking), Dr. Octagon (wicked), Loomis (Loomie!), Nathaniel Thane (outstanding! I'll never OD on you again, promised), Rinnan (forgive Evie, she was young and impressionable *grin*), Kingfox (for helping out), Chali (for the ink you did), all Evie's sisters in the VF (we rocked!).

All the other citizens of New Carthage and the players of Cybersphere, past and present. I didn't mention you all by name, I know, I know... And I probably forgot *points* you! When I get back, the first drink is on me. A special thanks goes to all the wizards, builders, GM's and other bits who built CS and kept it going all those years... much obliged. A big thanks also to everyone out there who took the time and effort to reply to my questionnaire.

Sander (thanks for thinking and writing with me... this is for you too), Christian (thanks for everything), Mariska (the crucial spark was yours and the little light has never died), Alan (for everything, love), everyone on Cybermind (for the inspiring conversations), Angela (loved role-playing for science's progress), Anna (for understanding I needed time for thinking... but not too much *grin*).

And last, but certainly not least, Jelle (someday we'll role-play together), Jef and Madeleen (for always supporting me in every way).

Frank Schaap

Glossary

. (pose)	A period is the symbol for the pose command; see **Pose.**
: (emote)	The colon is the symbol for the emote command; see **Emote.**
<brackets>	Pointy brackets are used to indicate commands (and data) as they are to be entered exactly. For an example see **Pose.**
@	The @ precedes commands that effect some change on the MOO. Thus <@brief> sets the output of all descriptions to brief mode, while <@verbose> sets them to verbose. Commands such as <smile> or <open> have the character perform an action and are thus not preceded by the @ sign.
AD&D	Advanced Dungeons & Dragons; see D&D. A newer version of the D&D role-playing game with a more advanced game system.
Admin	A "player" with an administrative function; see **Bit.**
Alt	An "alt" is an alternative emanation of a player. The admin on Cybersphere "wear" a certain guise when they are in their function as an admin, but they also have a character, an alt, in order to be able to partake in the role-playing as their character.
BBS	The Bulletin Board System. A virtual in-game bulletin board, serving both IC and OOC uses, where players can read and post messages under such categories as Meta (an OOC forum) and Want-Ads or Chat; IC forums are to be used for exchanges between characters, not players.
Bit	A "player" with an administrative function (wizard, builder, game-master) is called a "bit", because they have a flag (a bit) set on their character-object which tells the MOO that they have certain special privileges (such as being able to program on the MOO).
Bot	A non-player character animated by a simple "artificial intelligence" program, usually shopkeepers or bartenders.
BTW	By The Way

Character	The character is the player's "representation" in the virtual world.
CMC	Computer Mediated Communication
Complant	"Complant" is short for "communications implant", a device implanted in every citizen of New Carthage that allows them to access the local BBS and to send messages to other people "online" at that time.
CS	CyberSphere
Cybersphere	The name of the MOO that was my main fieldwork site.
D&D	Dungeons & Dragons.
DM	Dungeon Master, a "referee" in Fine's (1983) terms.
Emote	Generic term for the performance of an action by the character through use of the "emote" command. The emote command requires the player to input the desired action in the third person singular, <:nods pensively and scratches his chin.> results in the MOO parsing, "Character nods pensively and scratches his chin." Also see **Pose**.
GM	Game Master, a "referee" in Fine's (1983) terms.
IC	In Character.
ICly	Adverb meaning "in an In Character way".
IMHO	In My Humble Opinion
Log	Function of the MUD client that lets a player save the text of a role-playing session on disk.
Meta	"Meta" is one of the forums of the BBS on Cybersphere, where players can exchange OOC messages.
MOO	MUD, Object Oriented.
MUD	MUD originally stood for Multi User Dungeon. Alternative translations are Multi User Domain and Multi User Dimension.
MUD client	The program that runs on the player's computer, providing access to the MUD. A MUD client is just a fancy TELNET client.
New Carthage	The fictive city that is the center of the Cybersphere universe, previously known as Night City, modeled loosely after San Diego, USA.
NPC	Non Player Character, a character not animated by a player but either by a simple "artificial intelligence" (in which case it's called a "bot") or animated by a "referee" so that s/he can help and guide the action of hir tiny-plot.
Object	The basic building block from which the MOO is constructed.

OOC	Out Of Character.
OOCly	Adverb meaning "in an Out Of Character way."
Page	An instant message for another player. On Cybersphere pages can be both IC and OOC.
Player	The flesh-and-blood person behind the keyboard who animates a character.
Plot	A story line. Since there is no overarching plot to the MUD, role play takes place either ad-hoc, or organized around so called "tiny-plots", that are organized by the "referees" with and for the players.
Pose	The pose command is akin to the "emote" command, in that it lets the player perform an action through/for hir character. The player provides input in the first person singular and every verb that should be conjugated for the subject's point of view is to be preceded by a single period. <.laugh and .cry> results in the MOO parsing, "Character laughs and cries".
Referee	A referee in Fine's (1983) work on table-top role-playing games is the participant organizing and administrating the role-playing session. The referee takes care of thinking up and describing the fantasy environment and the narrative structure of the role-playing session. As the "author" of this particular instance of the game, the referee holds the power to decide on all matters not resolved by the role of the dice.
RP	Role-Play(ing).
RPG	Role-Playing Game.
Spivak	A gender-neutral gender available in many MUDs, resulting in a character with the following pronouns: e, em, eir, eirs, eirself.
Splat	A gender-neutral gender available in many MUDs, resulting in a character with the following pronouns: *e, h*, h*, h*s, h*self.
TELNET	A standard communications protocol that allows two computers to set up an interactive communications channel, for example giving the user of computer A access to a MUD running on computer B or the command line interface of computer B.
Tiny-plot	See Plot.

Introduction

> Our modern world has few, if any, frontiers. We can no longer escape to the frontier of the West, explore Darkest Africa, sail to the South Seas. Even Alaska and the Amazon Jungles will soon be lost as wild frontier areas. Furthermore, adventures are not generally possible anymore... It is therefore scarcely surprising that a game which directly involves participants in a make-believe world of just such nature should prove popular.
>
> —E. G. Gygax in Gary Alan Fine, *Shared Fantasy*

The journey is not just about getting to know a strange land and understanding the Other and his culture, it is also, and maybe more importantly, a way to better understand the Self, one's own country and culture. The journey provides the traveller with the experiences and the context that allow him to regard himself as in a mirror, as if he were not himself, but an Other. It is this distancing effect of "the mirror that reflects only inasmuch as it distorts" (Tyler 1987: 8) that temporarily suspends the traveller's common sense everyday reality and allows him to reflect on the axiomatic givens of his own culture in the safe knowledge that there is a plane waiting to take him home. Before the arrival of widespread (air)travel and TV, it was the anthropologist's task to tell the tales of strange lands, strange peoples and their customs, so that the reader could experience, at least in his imagination, what it would be like to live "there" and what it meant to have to look at his own everyday life as "other". The anthropologist now takes the same commercial flight as the tourist to the West, Darkest Africa, the South Seas, Alaska and the Amazon Jungles, but paradoxically the anthropologist's task hasn't changed much since the second half of the nineteenth century. If those faraway places are no longer unknown territories because you've already seen them on TV, in the brochure or the coffee table book (Mitchell 1989; Little 1990), then how can you see anything other in the mirror than what you already know when you go there? The anthropologist's task then, it would seem, is still to hold up the mirror, to tell the tale of another world, populated by other people in such a way that the reader can see himself, differently.

This is the tale of a journey into the worlds and lives of people who never live more than a few hundred milliseconds away because their second home is a role-playing MUD on the Internet. The MUDs that I will be discussing are text-based virtual environments, where multiple users meet, converse and interact in the semi-fictitious surroundings of their virtual world.[1] I will explain in more detail how MUDs technically work shortly,

> [b]ut suffice it to say, for now, that in practical terms, the experience of participating in a [MUD] is that one sits at a keyboard, in front of a screen, and projects oneself over a global computer network into an entirely textual world, and into an entirely virtual community. (Unsworth n.d.: n.p.)

That projection of oneself into the MUD takes the form of a "character" and by taking on that character's role, by "role-playing", you become one of the inhabitants of a virtual world. There are many different MUDs accessible over the Internet[2] and depending on the popularity of the MUD, your character will find itself amidst a dozen to a few hundred other characters. All these characters are played by as many players scattered around the world, all logging in to that virtual world at the same time. The term "player" is used throughout this text to refer to the actual, flesh and blood person behind the keyboard and the term "character" denotes the virtual representation of the player in the MUD. Although getting there is nearly instantaneous, every time the player logs in to the MUD, he metaphorically travels to another world. A world that usually doesn't claim to offer the player more than fun and diversion while he is there, playing his character, but that nevertheless is something more than an electronic Disneyland; the connotation of "virtual" in "virtual world" and "virtual reality" often is that of unreality, instead of non-physicality.

"Playing" a character in a MUD is more than just a game. Players indicate that they enjoy playing in the MUD because it usually is fun and MUDs certainly employ game elements to create an interesting environment for the players, but the whole "game" revolves not around winning, but around the social relations and social interactions between the characters. The interactions are real even though they are "played out" through the characters, in the sense that they are invented by, extended to and exchanged between the players. Although the virtual environment offers its own set of freedoms and limitations for interaction, a player needs all his social, cultural and linguistic knowledge and wits to convincingly and credibly perform his character. Part of that performance is convincingly presenting your character as male or female. This is easier said than done in a world where the performer has only text at his or her disposal. Since the player's physical body is not accessible in the MUD, the performance of the character is not automatically grounded by a 'naturally' gendered body. More difficult still, when other players scrutinize that performance because you might be "gender-bending". And just *who* is that ravishing blonde at the bar? She sure is smiling sweetly at you...

This study takes the performance of gender in/on/through the characters in a role-playing MUD as its central subject and aims to illustrate the processes by which cultural patterns and social conventions about gender and identity structure social interaction in MUDs. The analysis focuses on the different strategies employed by the players to present a convincing and credible male or female character and the strategies they employ to recognize "cross-gender" characters. A cross-gender character is a character with a gender opposite to that of the player. Besides taking on the male or female gender, MUDs allow the player to choose a non-conventional and/or gender-neutral gender for his character. "Gender bending" is the usual catchall term employed to refer to unorthodox applications of gender, both online and offline. The particularities of an online setting such as a MUD offer the researcher an interesting view on how social constructions such as gender take shape and structure social interaction in the absence of the physical body. A physical body that because of its sheer materiality often obscures the processes that make it meaningful in the social world. Keeping in line with the ambiguities of gender in an online setting, from this point in the text on I will use "hir" (a contraction of his and her) and "s/he" as convenient, somewhat gender neutral pronouns.[3] Instead of using another set of gender-neutral pronouns, such as for instance the spivak pronouns ("e, em, eir, eirs, eirself"), I choose these pronouns because they imply both a certain sense of gender neutrality *and* remind the reader of the 'natural' gender dichotomy in everyday life. Gender in everyday life after all is not changed or neutralized by a few keystrokes and has real effects and consequences for the way people live their lives.

The MUD is an example of real-time or synchronous computer-mediated communication, which means that even though players' utterances are typed out/in, they in many ways resemble the spoken, rather than the written word. In order to set the "text from the screen" apart from the "other text", I use a `monotype courier font` which is a common screen font. When quoting from interviews or role-playing situations I have corrected the most obvious typos, but I have left the original grammatical construction and punctuation as it was. Typos such as "viewer" misspelled as "veiwer", for example, I usually correct for readability, like most of the "uhs", "ehms" and false starts are left out of interviews transcribed from tape when they're not meaningful. Players often use several, usually trailing periods to indicate pauses in their "speech" or an unfinished thought. Trailing periods in the quotes therefore do not indicate the omission of a word or a sentence; my changes in the quotes (apart from the corrected typos) are always indicated by [square brackets], omissions are indicated by periods within square brackets [...]. In this book I use the character's "real" name where I have obtained permission to do so. Other characters I refer to by pseudonyms. I regularly refer to both the player and the character using the character's name, mirroring the general in-game practice, but where it is important to distinguish between the two I usually refer to the player with "character_name's player".

Scientific and novelistic discourses appear together in this book, trying to pick a path through ethnography's task of giving the reader an impression of the experience of living in another world, of playing a character in a MUD. The MUD could be understood as a collaborative effort in storytelling, with all the players playing their part in an unscripted, open ended, interactive and ad hoc novel. Together the players craft a tale where fact and fiction meet in an ever-expanding dialogical ebb and flood of textual exchanges. This book cannot be an accurate rendering of the dialogical form the characters and their world take, for that is reserved to the moment in which they are lived by the players. The novelistic and scientific prose attempt to evoke the ambiguous experience of "being there", the player living in text, the character simultaneously stirring the body's emotions and the anthropologist observing, not all that detached from the actual and virtual circumstances. The two main stories intertwined in this book tell, however partial(ly), the tale of my main character and the ethnographic inquiry of the role-playing MUD she lives in.

The structure of this book follows that of the classic ethnography, in the sense that in the first chapter it introduces the reader to the setting of the research in a more personal, descriptive section, after which the reader is informed of more technical aspects of that community such as lay of the land, transportation, demographics, etc. The second chapter then deals with the underlying theoretical framework and methodological issues. The third chapter presents the analysis and the case material as a "thick description" (Geertz 1973), the interpretation and the case material intertwined in the attempt to set down not just the spoken word, but what was said. The fourth and final chapter takes the discussion to the level of theory again, reflecting on the questions the material poses and the consequences it has for the theory. But there is a twist here to the classical approach. As Geertz noted in a later work, the personal and descriptive introduction is not just a sympathetic way to introduce the setting and the community to the reader, it also is a rhetorical ploy to convince the reader that the author really has been "there", to claim the authority of the "eyewitness" for the author (cf. Geertz 1988; Hendriks & Schaap 1995).

> The ability of anthropologists to get us to take what they say seriously has less to do with either a factual look or an air of conceptual elegance than it has with their capacity to convince us that what they says is a result of their having actually penetrated (or, if you prefer, been penetrated by) another form of life, of having, one way or another, truly "been there". And that, persuad-

> ing us that this offstage miracle has occurred, is where the writing comes in. (Geertz 1988: 4-5)

After the personal introduction, the rhetorical importance of which is often overseen, the voice of the author disappears from the classical ethnography and what remains is the seemingly objective and scientific account, free of troubling signs of subjectivity. Tyler, after Bacon, calls the language of the objective and scientific account "Plain Style", "[the] utopian dream of transparent language, of language so perfectly fitted to the world that no difference could insinuate itself between words and things" (Tyler 1987: 7). Plain Style eschews the use of rhetoric, because "[r]hetoric is the mark of the author's will, and all allusion, allegory, metaphor, simile and ornaments of style are its instruments" (ibid.: 8). The form this text takes hopefully reminds the reader that Plain Style itself is a rhetorical form and where this text, inevitably it seems, tends towards authorless authority I hope to have provided a strong enough counter voice. The form and structure of the argument are as important as what is argued, because they define the frame of analysis in which the argument functions. Travel and exploration are important metaphors for structuring argument, knowledge and understanding (Lakoff & Johnson 1980) and, true to form then, this journey begins with arriving.

CHAPTER 1

Setting the Scene

Arriving

I was nobody. A clone with a number. The city was big, dangerous and very new to me. With nowhere to run, the city would chew me up and spit me out, eventually. In the mean time it was up to me to go with the flow, to stay one step ahead of trouble and its speeding bullet. I could feel that I'd become part of the city's cycle of life and death. The throbbing bustle of people wheeling and dealing, shouting and whispering, fighting and loving seeped in through the thin lucite walls. Somehow I had found my way into a sleeping coffin in a cube hotel the night before and now my back was complaining about the thin foam padding, my skin sore from the paper Salvation Army zipsuit. Lying on my back, my eyes half closed, almost comfortable, I pulled up some factsheets about New Carthage. Somehow I always suspected the communications implant to buzz or click or make noises by itself in the back of my head, but nothing of that kind happened, of course. The neurologically hooked up complant in my head conveyed the images and text directly to the appropriate parts of my brain and I browsed through the data I had plucked from the city's public net. Disconnected, as if regarding myself from a distance, I lay there for a while, considering my options. I knew why I had come here, but feeling the cold oppressiveness of the city all around me, I wondered how realistic pursuing my dream was and whether the city would kill me underfoot as a bug for trying to live up to that dream.

Quite pronounced a message flooded into my consciousness, a sure sign that my complant was visible on the public net. The message came from someone who called himself Mad Hatter. He had noticed that I still didn't have a name on the comnet, just the generic clone-message. Maybe he was bored, but whatever his reasons were, he apparently was interested in someone new to the city, as he offered me some help getting to know my way around the city. I agreed to come out of the coffin as soon as I had braced myself for the outside world. After a few minutes of silent contemplation I had still not changed the clone-message on the comnet and Mad Hatter asked me if I was a man or a woman. I laughed and told him my name was Eveline and that I was a woman.

He grinned and asked me if I was going to stay in the coffin for much longer. He had to go somewhere in a while.

I changed my comnet ID to Eveline and taking one last deep breath, I kicked the little door at my feet open and slid out of the coffin. I looked around. The coffin platform wasn't too big and peering up at the sky I thought I even saw some direct sunlight filtering through the chemically colored clouds. A plain looking guy, dressed casually in a pair of Levi's and black leather jacket stepped forward from the shadows of the far end of the platform. The spiked dog collar around his neck and the spiked bracers on his forearms conveyed the message "street-wise" rather convincingly. As I stood there, watching him walk up to me, I figured that I had to start somewhere and it might as well be here, with trusting this guy.

He ruffled my hair and said, "Eveline? Follow me."

The way he said that made it sound not like a question, but the most normal thing in the world to say, just like the way he ruffled my hair was the most normal thing in the world to do. At least he made it seem like it was. I nodded and followed him down the iron spiral staircase, into the pungent smell of cigarettes, liquor and sweat. Reaching the last step of the stairs my eyes had accommodated to the low level of light here. Neon beer and liquor ads were the only source of light and while the whole bar was rather dimly lit to say the least, most people seemed to prefer the even darker corners and booths for their conversations. The only two people that I could really see were a man and a woman sitting together at the bar. A bluish neon glow illuminated their faces through the mirror behind the bar. The woman was concentrating on a little vial, filling a syringe with the liquid it contained. She then spread the fingers of her left hand apart and jabbed the needle into the flesh between her index and middle finger. Biting her lip she emptied the syringe into her bloodstream.

"Fuck," she muttered and licked away the blood that was beading up between her fingers.

"Yeah, well... that stinks eh?" the man drawled.

I turned and saw Mad Hatter motioning for me to follow him into the dark back room of the bar. Brushing my hair back I nodded to Mad Hatter and wondered why the little scene at the bar had caught my eye the way it did. If I'd ever dream about it I would probably be able to read what it said on the label of the little vial. I looked over my shoulder at the man and the woman at the bar and saw the woman carefully put the vial and the syringe into a little leather roll-up container.

"Tell me about it... my friend had to be shipped off back east to some mental hospital to get her mind straight after that," the woman said to the man without looking up from her busy hands.

Weaving my way through the crowd I left the man and the woman at the bar behind and followed Mad Hatter into the back room. The only light here was the soft neon glow filtering in from the bar and the glare of a huge and very old television set. The TV was showing a news channel with the sound muted, something about a guy who had lost both arms in some sort of boostergang attack. The ceiling dipped so low that you could actually touch it and a jukebox was pounding techno through a set of damaged loudspeakers. Given the general public's preferences for dark, out of the way spots the backroom surprisingly enough was empty. I followed Mad Hatter past an unoccupied sofa and he quickly shattered the window in the north wall of the back room, cupping his hand in his jacket. Reaching through the broken glass he opened the window and climbed through.

"Come on," he urged me from the other side.

I put my hands on the windowsill and jumped through, landing in a foul smelling alley. Garbage and debris lay heaped in huge piles against the walls and I covered my nose to ward off the stench.

"This is really horrible," I muttered as I walked over to Mad Hatter.

"Shoot! Empty," he said, kicking at a big crate in the least smelly corner of the alley. "Usually you can get some more or less decent clothes from this crate here, but it seems someone beat us to it. Well, I hope they're happy with it." He grinned. "Come on, back the way we came."

"Bummer," I said, although I didn't really mean it. We climbed back through the window. I sure was hoping I could find something more decent to wear than some rags someone had left in a crate in a smelly alley. On the other hand, now that I was starting to sweat a little, the paper zipsuit was starting to scratch and itch even more. I followed Mad Hatter back into the bar. The man and the woman were still sitting at the bar, their hushed conversation stopping as we entered. As we reached the door a sturdy man in a trench coat walked in. He glared at me with dark eyes as he pushed past us, grumbling, "Fucking perverted drones."

With a sigh of relief I stepped outside, only to feel dwarfed by the immensity of the city and the crowds on the street. Right next to the entrance the remains of a police drone with massive damage to the engine area leaned against the wall. A setting sun dyed the city red, the last rays of light dripping down the dead drone. Punkers, zoners, cromags and even quite some rather normal looking people pushed their way past, only casually glancing at the dead drone, if at all. I realized that I had slept right through most of the day and that I had found my way downtown last night, when it had been much quieter. Mad Hatter grabbed my hand and pulled me across the sidewalk and onto the street, where the cars, trikes and bikes were inching along in a cloud of exhaust fumes, honking horns and curses in at least five different languages.

"Come on! We ain't got all day," he shouted over his shoulder as we dodged a big van that suddenly saw the opportunity to lunge forward at least half a metre.

Mad Hatter dragged me along on the sidewalk, through the push and pull of the crowd, dodging the wide-open arms of a preacher with an artificial halo and quickly sidestepping a smoking manhole without a lid. We ducked around a corner and then hurried down a street that was bathing in the glow of holosigns. The shops lining the street were offering everything, and probably more, you'd care to buy. Without letting go of his hand we dodged across another congested street. This side of street stood in stark contrast to the other side. Banks, real estate agencies and posh shops politely invited customers inside their enormous well-kept buildings.

Mad Hatter waved unceremoniously with his hand and explained, "The moneywall..."

Automated doors swished open and he led us into a bank, appropriately called Bancorp Financial Services. The air in here smelled vaguely of synthetics in the slow waft of ceiling fans.

"Use one of those terminals to open an account here." Mad Hatter grinned, "It's really the only bank that does business with people like us."

The terminals were easy enough to use alright. A thumb scan and a retinal scan were all that it took to open the account. The terminal spat out a personalized credstick and the Nippon Welfare Fund donated 200 credits, all in a matter of seconds. I took the credstick from the slot and put my thumb against the sensor plate. The credstick displayed the Bancorp logo and the balance of 200 creds in lo-glo lettering. I smiled, thinking that things might turn out not quite as bad as I had thought and walked back to Mad Hatter, who was waiting next to an impressive info-column.

"Okay, I've got a credstick and 200 creds now..."

"Right, clothes and some advantages are next on your list then, " Mad Hatter said.

"Advantages?"

"Yeah, with the stick come insurance creds that you can use to get implants. You'll need those," he replied matter of factly as he took my hand again, heading for the exit.

I tried to think about the implications of having to get cybernetic implants as we hurried down the more civilized and airy side of the street and then crossed back to the darker, more crowded side of the street at the first junction. I noticed that respectable but simple shops lined the street here and Mad Hatter slowed down a little but we still got ahead fast, since it was getting less and less crowded here. I had lost all sense of direction by now and I just knew that we were heading west, judging by the setting sun. So far I had always managed to get by without chipping in and I couldn't quite make up my mind about the implants. It was like adding a piece of a machine to yourself, but you couldn't really see it. The complant had turned out to be quite a handy little thing, and besides, it just enhanced you, right? Mad Hatter opened the door of an old, but decent looking shop for me and I snapped out of my pensive mood.

"Thanks," I smiled at him.

"After you," he grinned.

The shop had Maggs Creations stenciled across the window and a woman smiled warmly at us as we entered before returning to her sewing. I started looking through the clothing on the racks and looked up when I heard the shopkeeper say to Mad Hatter, "That sheer negligee goes for 50 creds."

"Now really..." I said to Mad Hatter.

He just grinned and put the negligee back on the rack. "Okay, pick out some clothes you like and we'll get out of here."

After some consideration I picked a black pair of jeans, a purple silk shirt and some plain cotton underwear. I waved to Mad Hatter, who was still inspecting underwear and flimsy see-through garments and went into the fitting room with the clothes. When I came out with my new clothes on I couldn't help but sighing with relief, "Ah... almost human again."

Mad Hatter handed me a pair of stiletto heeled boots and looked me up and down, "Nice... these will be the finishing touch."

I don't like high heels, but I didn't feel like I could reject his offer. He had already bought me all the clothes and these boots too, because everything was way more expensive than I could afford. So I just smiled and put on the boots. Feeling my confidence returning with the new clothing and standing so much taller in those stilettos I walked up to Mad Hatter and pecked him on the cheek.

"Thanks," I said as I watched him blush a little.

"That's okay... now let's get you those advantages," he replied.

We left the shop, back to the streets and again I was struck by the sheer size of the city, the fact that I didn't have a clue where I was and whether I was ever going to find my way back to the safe sleeping coffins. We crossed the street, dodging through the traffic and before I knew it, we were in the lobby of something that once had been a clinic. I hesitated again at the thought of artificial augmentation of my body, but Mad Hatter didn't stop and led me through a door into the smell of aether.

Mad Hatter pointed to a rather unshaven, shabby looking older guy lying on the operating table, "And that's Doc Benway..."

The Doc got up, looked us over and still a bit groggily started a lecture on the blessings of implants. The big pricelist on the wall showed a range of products, from direct neural interfaces to grafted muscles and razorclaws. I looked around, studying the pricelist, my doubts getting bigger as the Doc rambled on about enhanced human capabilities. Then Mad Hatter raised his voice and interrupted the Doc.

"Doc? Doc... listen. It's for the lady. She needs the basics to stay alive or at least put up some resistance. I guess basic grafted muscles and dermal armor would do the trick for her. She's got insurance creds..."

The Doc muttered something about niceties and courtesy, but motioned me to lie down on the now vacant operating table, so I did. A shiver ran down my spine.

"Listen here, miss... this is nanotech, you won't feel a thing but a little itching for the first coupla days. Don't exercise too hard those first coupla days till all the tech has sunk in properly and attached itself to your biological tissues, 'kay?" the Doc said to me. I could smell the alcohol in his breath.

The Doc rolled a trolley with a couple of battered cylinders and tubes over to the operating table and rolled up my sleeve. He punched keys on the terminal on the trolley for a minute or so and then grabbed one of the tubes and fixed a fresh needle on the end. He took my bare arm and slapped it a few times, bringing out the veins. I looked the other way and felt the needle slip into my vein. The Doc started tapping at the terminal again and in fifteen minutes the whole operation was over. The Doc swiped my credstick through the slot on the wall console and then waved us out. Back on the street I noticed being lightheaded and itchy indeed, the smell of aether in Doc Benway's had probably just added to the feeling.

"Are you hungry?" Mad Hatter asked.

"Yeah," I replied, thinking something to eat should help getting rid of the lightheadedness. I hadn't really eaten in two days, not counting the soyburger I had last night.

"Well, then follow me, madam."

I smiled up at him, "Of course..."

I took Mad Hatter's proffered arm, happy that things were still going smoothly while I had expected so much trouble. I figured I owed Mad Hatter big time. Again we headed into the maelstrom of people and traffic that filled the streets in the last light of the day. The neon and lo-glo glimmered overhead and underfoot and rush-hour added to the madness. It was quite a walk before we reached a place called *The Intrigue.* The entrance gave way to a big room filled with slot machines. The wood paneling and the plush carpeting effectively dampened the noise from the machines. Someone had actually given the room and its layout quite some thought, the only way to cross it was past the most inviting and seductive of the machines. The next room was even spacier, a bar lining one side and various gambling tables, adequately lit by lamps hanging from the high ceiling, taking up the rest of the space. Nearly all the tables were occupied by one or more players and the quiet rustle of cards, dices and ice cubes in glasses accompanied the voices that asked for another card or a raise filled the room. Leaving the gambling behind we entered the restaurant in the back of the casino through a short, but dark corridor. The waiter welcomed us courteously and showed us to our table in the back of the tastefully decorated restaurant.

Mad Hatter pulled out the chair for me and sat me down with a friendly, "After you..."

I winked at him, "Either you are a gentleman or you play one very convincingly."

He smiled and studied the menu, "What are you having?"

"Hmmm, they don't have toast and scrambled eggs, so I'll have the spaghetti then. Doesn't mix very well with Earl Grey, but I could use a cup," I said.

Mad Hatter ordered two spaghettis and two Earl Grey teas from the waiter. The speed with which the order was served made me wonder about the size of the microwave the kitchen was featuring. Mad Hatter linked credsticks with the waiter and I dug in hungrily. Actually, the spaghetti was pretty good. The food was getting most of my attention, so during dinner we only discussed where we both were from, originally. I shoved the plate away when I was done and leaned back in my chair, surveying the mess of red sauce we had left on the table. I grinned and Mad Hatter took another clean napkin and made a sailor's hat out of it. He leaned forward and placed it on my head.

I smiled, "Too bad we didn't go for a sailor's shirt in that shop."

Mad Hatter grinned, "Indeed. I have to go though, shall I walk you back to your coffin?"

I nodded and finished the last of my tea. Mad Hatter got up and courteously pulled the chair back for me. We made our way back to the entrance of the restaurant and the waiter thanked us profusely for our visit. Stepping into the darkness of the short corridor I suddenly felt Mad Hatter's hands on me. All over me. He pretended to tickle me, but it was obvious that his intentions were otherwise. I panicked. I got loose and turned away, managing a feeble, "You eeky... don't tickle me," but that wasn't what I meant.

I didn't know the town. I didn't know where I was or where I could run to. I didn't know the people or their rules. I didn't know the first thing about Mad Hatter and I felt him tackle me again and pin me down. My heart went cold. I turned myself loose from his grip, again, and in the coldest and most resolute voice I could muster I said, "No dirty tricks here, buster."

I could feel him stare at me, his eyes hidden in the darkness and I was surprised with my own voice, still ringing in my ears. For a moment that took forever we just stood there, until he said, "Where can I escort you to?"

Keeping myself together I said, "That's better... can you escort me back to the coffins?"

He nodded and we walked back to the cube hotel. My whole body and mind wired, I was ready to jump at the slightest, but nothing happened. We didn't speak. Up on the cube platform Mad Hatter just took a key from the dispenser and crawled into a coffin, leaving me behind to stare at the rows of dirty aluminium doors. I took a key too and got into a coffin as far away from his as I could. I lay awake in my coffin for a long time, the city, that day and my future milling through my head. When I finally slept, I dreamed.

Cybersphere

> I must have dreamed myself astray
> The only milkyway I have, is in the middle of the day
> —Neneh Cherry, *Somedays*

The previous section is an account of the first day I spent in a role-playing MUD, a "virtual world" on the Internet. It is quite a literal rendering of what happened that day, based on the log and my personal experience of that session. I have used the dialogue from the log literally and the "words spoken by the characters" thus were actually "spoken" that fateful day.[4] For more than two years I spent up to sixteen hours a day, almost every day, role-playing my character on a MUD. Before I started my research I had never played on a MUD nor had I ever played a pen-and-paper Role-Playing Game (RPG), but I knew more or less what to expect because of my longstanding fascination with computers, Internet, and the cyberpunk and fantasy genres. Josh Quittner's article *Johnny Manhattan Meets the Furry Muckers* in Wired magazine (1994) eventually made me so curious that I searched out a friendly MUD and logged on.[5] Quittner describes his first experiences on one of the biggest virtual worlds around, LambdaMOO. As I later discovered from my own experiences and other literature, the article can be read as fairly exemplary of 'first contact' with a social virtual world. The article also details Quittner's interesting visits to a world called *FurryMUCK*, which is populated by (often anthropomorphic) animals and humans with animal-like qualities. The most salient aspect of this particular world that Quittner picks up on is that these 'animals' are having virtual sex with one another in most intriguing ways. Quittner wisely leaves most details to the reader's imagination, but he sparked my anthropological interest in these virtual worlds where everything seems possible, even such bizarre happenings as 'animals' having virtual sex.

At the outset of the research I thought I would do an "old fashioned" community study and write an ethnography about this hitherto largely unresearched area and its strange and intriguing inhabitants. The enormity of such a project slowly dawned upon me, as I got more and more involved in one virtual world in particular. It became clear that I would have to narrow down my research questions and restrict my research to a more defined and limited area of research. One thing that is rather hard to miss, as a novice to online role-playing, is that when you create your character there are several options to choose from besides "male" and "female" for the gender of your character. The option "neuter" is rather self-explanatory, but options like "spivak", "plural" and "splat" indicate that gender online might just be something a bit different from what it is offline, in Real Life (IRL).

Indeed, a lot of the early studies on Computer Mediated Communication (CMC) and online social interaction in one way or another deal with the fact that in CMC there usually is no access to the physical body of one's "dialogical partner", which means that online you can enjoy a certain degree of anonymity, which means that online you can present a character that doesn't have to mesh with your offline identity, which means that you can also present a character that is of another gender than your Real Life gender (some of the more influential early articles would be: Bruckman 1992; Cherny 1994; Curtis 1992; Danet 1996; Dibbell 1993; Reid 1994; Stone 1995; Turkle 1995). Especially the fact that as your character you can assume a non-conventional gender seems an intriguing possibility/materialization of the postmodern sentiments in society and science. MUDs are text-based and choosing a non-conventional gender for your character means that the MUD program will apply all the relevant pronouns when your character interacts with other players or objects in the MUD. The neuter gender for example has the more familiar pronouns "it, its, itself" associated with it, while the spivak gender will generate the pronouns "e, em, eir, eirs, eirself." The plural gender comes with the pronouns "they, them, their, theirs, themselves" and the splat gender is associated with the purely textual and thus unpronounceable pronouns "*e, h* ,h* ,h*s ,h*self."[6] Gender thus presented itself as an intriguing subject for my study, specific enough to stay on track and wide enough to allow me to explore related aspects of identity and community online.

Eventually I decided to look at how players present a convincingly gendered body for the character they are playing and how they incorporate particular cultural patterns in their performance of gender. To research the performance of gender in MUDs, I have focused solely on role-playing MUDs where the players actually play human figures. Although it would be fascinating to research concepts of gender among those who play Furries, as a social anthropologist I am interested first and foremost in the way the concepts of gender are performed on or through human characters. A second reason that I have chosen to limit myself to role-playing MUDs is that, in my opinion, they provide the most elaborate and sustained construction of a virtual reality and offer the most elaborate individual character building. In order to indicate the scope and depth these text-based virtual realities have for their inhabitants I also refer to them as "virtual worlds."

In his wonderfully detailed monograph on pen-and-paper RPGs, entitled *Shared Fantasy: Role-Playing Games as Social Worlds,* Gary Alan Fine underscores the extensiveness and engrossing character of the worlds created in role-playing when he writes that,

> [i]f the setting was all that was being created, our interest in the social components of fantasy would be misplaced. These are not only fantasy settings, but are *worlds* in which the game action takes place. (Fine 1983: 76, italics in original)

Generally the goal of role-playing is the playing itself. To play your character you have to be partial to the illusion of an Other world and you have to suspend your disbelief just like when immersing yourself in a good novel or a movie. Indeed, like Fine I feel I must underscore the importance of "engrossment" or "immersion" in these virtual worlds.

> For the game to work as an aesthetic experience players must be willing to "bracket" their "natural" selves and enact a fantasy self. They must lose themselves to the game. This engrossment is not total or continuous, but it is what provides the "fun" within the game. The acceptance of the fantasy world as a (temporarily) real world gives meaning to the game, and the creation of a fantasy scenario and culture must take into account those things that players find engrossing. (Fine 1983: 4)

The MOO that I eventually chose as the main "field site" for my research is called *Cybersphere,* a post-apocalyptic cyberpunk world. In the late 2020's, in the fictive city of New Carthage, people live in a harsh and dark world, dominated by merciless multinational corporations and local gangs. A series of smaller and bigger wars and conflicts has turned the world into a patchwork of more or less autonomous city-states and has divided New Carthage into two parts, the wealthy corporate sector behind the money wall and the sprawling, poor part of the city where people try to survive by joining a gang or seeking employment with one of the more or less legal branches of a corporation. Weapons, industrial espionage, drugs and sex make up the biggest part of New Carthage's economy and those dealing in high-tech will only talk to you if you can afford it. In this city you can get a clone, just in case... you can get dermal armor, great against backstabbing, or you could get a Direct Neural Interface, so you can access the matrix with a cyberdeck and learn how to enter corporate databanks to sell off the tasty bits. And amidst all this violence, all this fighting over power and money, people still try to live a somewhat normal life. It's easier to fall in love than to keep a relationship going, but some dare to challenge fate and marry, and even sometimes have children. In New Carthage you can live your life, from the smallest detail to the larger than life experience, with an amazing sense of reality.

My character lived in this city for over three years. In this violent city I have worked, eaten, slept, gotten drunk and fallen in love. I have loved and lost those I loved. I have killed to survive and barely survived the attack of a psychotic gang leader myself. My character is called Eveline and 'therefore' she is a woman. The other half of my divided self was being an anthropologist during that time, who registered what happened with his "forked eye" (cf. Tyler 1987: 91) and took notes. As an anthropologist I studied the daily life of the citizens of New Carthage as I might have done in any other town.

Dialing in

```
[-] [2945]---From: mr._simon at Tue Oct 27 9:03pm 2028---
[-] Subj: Addiction
[-] I hear the tones after the ring.
[-] Been close to 3years script still works; I have it loud
[-]  just the same.
[-] Chek the mail, surf the updates and see if UseNet still
[-]  houses only losers.
[-] I feel it twitch...I check the room.  Alone.
[-] Grab my gear..tweeked ZMUD code ported for the mac; its
[-]  blend of IRC and FTP excite me.
[-] The pause and hopeful gasp as I see the message of the
[-]  day...please no lag.
[-]
[-] I am in.
[-] Who
[-] There always the same.  A few first timers in way over
[-]  their head...I control the world.
[-] @@stats
[-] DAMN this drug really does nothing for me.
[-] The haze bleeds through my IRL vision...I am need not this
[-]  iMac.
[-] Take the stream and live the dream.  CyberFreaks unite and
[-]  join my unholy cry NCSP they might die.
[-] I think I can I think I can...DAMN.
[-] I can do it... where the hell is my support. Not now
[-]  later?  Its always later.
[-] Damn he has that?  NCSP imagine that!!.
[-] Clone. I am still alone.
[-] Another day they all will pay!!
[-] -------
```

—mr. simon, *Cybersphere*

simon's raw poetry kept me staring at the screen. The accuracy of his words tied my tummy in a knot, that awkward delight when your body reacts physically to a text. The modem chirps and whines as it forges a connection to the Net, a little daily *rite de passage.* The noise of the modem prepares the body for an other sort of experience. As the body settles and slows down, the senses re-adjust to a different kind of input, one that is a combination of feedback and evocation. Entering this digital realm, reaching out to the others that live there is best done alone. Alone in front of the screen. With no distractions the mind can reach down the wires, the keyboard's soft tapping the only sound. Or, alternatively, loud music blotting out everything else. If you're interested in such a thing and if you know where to look, you can enter one of the many virtual worlds that lie hidden behind one of the ports of certain nodes of the Net.

A MUD is a "text-based virtual reality" (Curtis 1992: 347) that is accessible in real time by multiple users over the Internet. Pavel Curtis, the author of LambdaMOO,[7] describes MUDs in his seminal 1992 article *MUDding: Social Phenomena in Text-based Virtual Realities* like this:

> A MUD is a software program that accepts "connections" from multiple users across some kind of network[8]... and provides each user access to a shared database of "rooms", "exits", and other objects. Each user browses and manipulates this database from "inside" one of those rooms, seeing only those objects that are in the same room and moving from room to room mostly via the exits that connect them. A MUD, therefore, is a kind of virtual reality, an electronically represented "place" that users can visit. (Curtis 1992: 347)

When you log on to a MUD you can usually visit as a guest character or you can create a character for yourself. Having a character is necessary to manifest oneself in that virtual world. The character is in a sense the player's virtual body that is able to move about and speak or manipulate objects in this virtual world. The virtual worlds I am speaking of here, are not made of lushly rendered three-dimensional graphical representations, rather, everything is presented through text. Walking into a room will display to the player a text stating that one has entered a room called, for instance, "A Shabby Downtown Bar", and a description of what can be seen there. A typical MUD consists of hundreds if not thousands of "rooms", ranging from toilets and elevators to large open spaces and vast factory halls. If other characters happen to be present a message will be displayed stating that, for instance, "Bob" is present. You can "look" at Bob to see the description of what he looks like and you can "speak" to Bob through your character by typing in the "say" command. The text following the "say" command will be echoed back to the player and it will be displayed to Bob. A more detailed and technical illustration of this sort of social interaction in a MUD follows shortly.

Originally the acronym MUD stood for *Multi User Dungeon,* MUDs being the plural form.[9] While the acronym MUD seems to be the most frequently used common denominator, several other acronyms and names are used to point out the differences between this particular MUD and the 'traditional' MUD. One of the most common other terms is MOO, which stands for *MUD Object Oriented* and it derives its name from the way its central program handles the "objects" of which the virtual world is composed. Another often used acronym is MUSH, which stands for *Multi User Shared Hallucination.* The key terms "multi" and "user" in all instances prompts some to write MU* (the asterisk being a wildcard) when pointing to all forms of virtual worlds. In this text I will try to restrict myself to the use of the term MUD, when referring in general to the different kinds of "Multi User Text-Based Virtual Realities." I will use the term MOO when I'm referring to MOO-code specific things. In the way I use the terms, the MOO software is thus a particular implementation of the general idea of the MUD, of which there are other implementations such as Diku, LP and MUSH. The MOO software is a program, a server that accepts connections and provides the players with the environment and the tools for their RP and other interactions.

MUDs find their origins in the pen-and-paper Role-Playing Games of which *(Advanced) Dungeons and Dragons* (AD&D) was and still is one of the most popular. AD&D and related role-playing games are usually set in a fantasy world that is often strongly influenced by J.R.R. Tolkien's epic tale *The Lord of the Rings.* To partake in an AD&D based role-playing game the player takes on the role of a character. The character is defined by various characteristics: its race (human, elven, orc, etc.), its gender (male, female, neuter), its class (mage, warrior, thief, etc.), a set of individual qualities (strength, intelligence, agility, endurance, etc.), and a set of personal skills (archery, magical and healing powers, etc.). These statistics are expressed numerically on the character's "stat-sheet" and will be evaluated by the roll of the dice. The goal of the game is to guide your character through an adventure as well as you can and to gain treasures, experiences and loot which can be used to "build", or to better your character's statistics. Hence, when you confront a monster and decide to fight it, your statistics are "rolled" against those of the monster: the dice and the current state of your character's statistics determine the outcome. In pen-and-paper role-playing games, which are played by a couple of people (usually some three to twelve persons) who are sitting around the table together, the adventure and the roll of the dice are governed by one of the participants called the Game Master (GM), Dungeon Master (DM) or "referee" in Fine's (1983) terms. In online AD&D based games the quests and the roll of the dice are usually maintained and supervised by subroutines of the MUD-program.

Three important and closely related differences between pen-and-paper role-playing games and their online counterparts must be noted. Firstly, in most online RPGs there is no referee as such and secondly, the players of online RPGs do not convene in a single physical locale to play the game, they rather log into the virtual world from their own study, dorm room, internet cafe, or wherever they have access to an internet connection. Thirdly, the fantasy world of a pen-and-paper RPG exists "in the moment", when the referee and the players convene, whereas online RPGs have a real and persistent existence in the form of a program, containing rooms, objects and characters, running on a computer even when individual players are not logged in. This has a serious impact on the way a player can become immersed in the virtual world. Fine shows how pen-and-paper role players ultimately partake in the referee's creation of a very idiosyncratic fantasy world and how the level of engrossment of the players is correlated with the referee's ability to describe, call up and control their fantasy world, channeling, so to speak, the players' individual fantasies into a coherent and shared fantasy whole. All information about this world comes only from the referee and s/he's the "God" who ultimately decides on the characters' faith.[10]

In an online RPG the role of the referee, if there's such a position at all, is quite different. Firstly, in pen-and-paper RPGs some 3 to 12, but usually 4 to 6 players take part (cf. Fine 1983: 175-176), while the number of active players on a MUD, depending on the hour of the day, can reach 30 or 40, with some MUDS reaching 150 to 200 active players at once. Secondly, in an online RPG neither the players, nor their characters are in the same physical or virtual locale. In an online RPG the referee would, were s/he able to monitor *all* the players at once, be completely swamped by a humongous amount of text, while the fact that the players are neither in the same physical or virtual locale as the referee would present insurmountable problems with regard to the referee's authority and hir ability to effect any changes or events that would be necessary for the game. In most online RPGs, instead of one plot played out by all the players, the bulk of the role-playing consists of "chance" encounters and the resulting spontaneous interactions between characters.

Usually there also is a series of concurrent Tiny-plots.[11] A Tiny-plot is a shorter or longer story line, organized by one of the referees and usually involving some 5 to 6 characters essential to the plot and another 5 or 6 peripheral characters. The referees take care of the advancement of their tiny-plot by deploying non-player characters (NPCs) that are involved in the plot at various, often strategic stages, and by making sure that rooms and objects essential to the plot have been build/programmed. A referee in an online RPG is however rarely in the position to govern *all* the action that takes place in hir tiny-plot and is thus involved in the plot on a much more fragmented basis than the referee of a pen-and-paper RPG. The whole of the online virtual world thus much less depends on an individual referee's imagination and refereeing skills than its pen-and-paper counterpart.[12] The individual players, the enactments of their characters, the chance encounters, and the relationships played out outside of organized plots are therefore much more important to the creation of an immersive and shared virtual world than in pen-and-paper RPGs.

The use and orientation of MUDs have diversified a lot since the late eighties and early nineties and "MUD" is now commonly translated with *Multi User Domain* or *Multi User Dimension.* Apart from AD&D based MUDs, usually called *fantasy* or *adventure* MUDs, one can find virtual worlds based on science fiction books, such as William Gibson's cyberpunk trilogy, or TV shows, such as *Star Trek* and *Babylon 5.* Some MUDs are based on cartoon characters such as the *X-men* or Japanese manga figures. Other MUDs offer the player an eclectic combination of different themes all meshed together and some MUDs get by without a definite theme at all. There are also MUDs that are used for long distance teaching and others are used for various sorts of scientific research and some MUDs merely provide a virtual social place where people can meet.

It is necessary to make a few crucial distinctions between different kinds of virtual worlds. In general I think that you can discern three different kinds of MUDs. Firstly, there are the traditional MUDs that are geared towards exploring, fulfilling quests and gaining treasures and experience points; these MUDs are usually fantasy MUDs and their game system is some derivation of the AD&D system. Secondly, there are social MUDs, where players convene mostly to chat and to build, that is to program, on their world; these MUDs usually don't feature a game system, since there are no adventures, no treasures and no experience points to be gained here. Thirdly, there are role-playing MUDs that offer a sustained role-playing environment and the players mostly convene there to role play; on these MUDs the administrators can choose to implement a game system, and if it is implemented it is usually modified to support role-playing, placing less importance on the slaying of monsters and gaining of gold. One shouldn't try to apply these categories too rigorously however, as boxing in is one of the things most mudders abhor, and in one way or another most MUDs seem to offer something out of each category anyway. The categories on the other hand *can* be used to determine the basic premises on which a specific MUD functions. The expectations raised by the dominant mode that the administrators set for their world define for a large part how players interact with one another and the MUD-environment on that particular MUD.

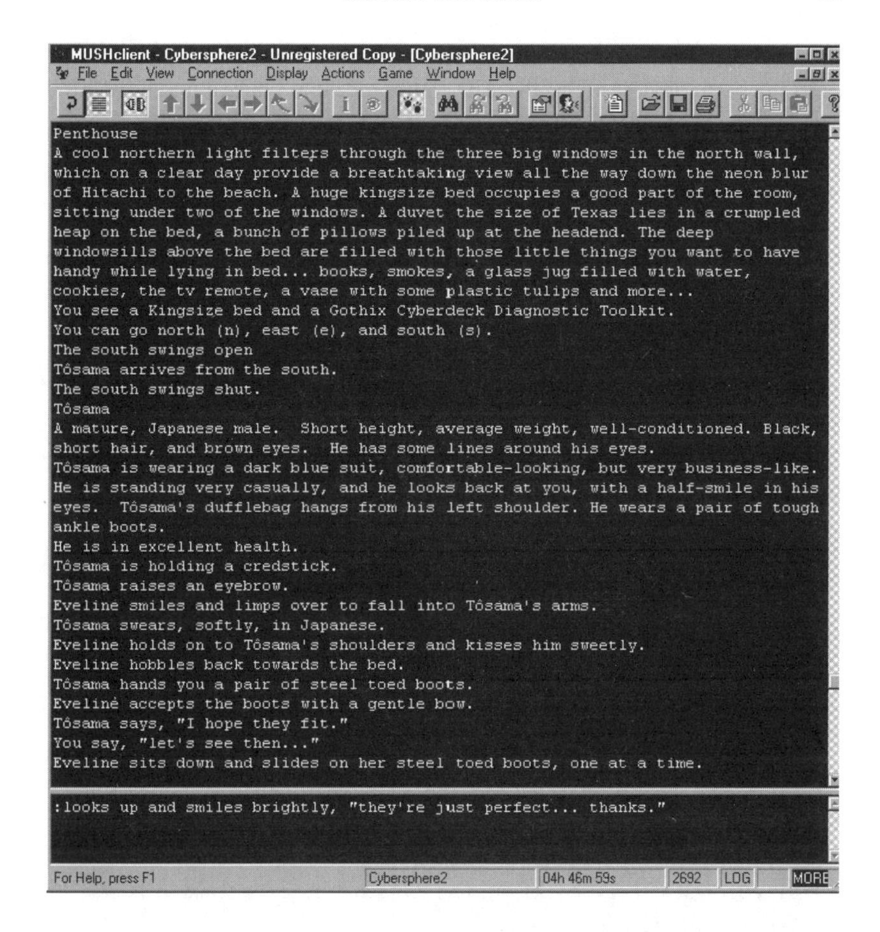

The most practical way to connect to a MUD is through a special purpose telnet program, a MUD-client. Figure 1 shows the user interface for such a program. The screen is divided into two text windows. The upper window, the output window, displays all the text that the MUD-program sends to the user. The lower window, the input window, is where the player can input and edit the commands and text s/he wants to send to the MUD. Once the player hits the enter key, the text displayed in the input window is send to the MUD. The MUD-program then parses the commands and executes them, sending the results back to the player, where the MUD-client will display them in the output window.

The player interacts with the objects and other players present in the MUD by typing in commands. In order to show what actually happens on the keyboard and the screen when one is submerged in the world of a MUD, let me explain in detail the scene displayed in Figure 1. The character that is played by me is called Eveline and the other character is called Tôsama. The text represents the point of view of Eveline. The commands that I have entered are indicated by the bold italic face in the explanation below. The commands that the player behind Tôsama entered are not shown because I, as a player, only get to see the resulting text of other players' commands. Usually the user can toggle an option whether the commands that s/he hirself enters should or shouldn't be echoed in the output window. Having your own commands echoed in the output window is a sort of safety measure: you read back what you have entered immediately and any mistakes can quickly be taken care of, albeit "after the fact."

The "`look`" command will display a description of the room one is currently in. This description has been written by the programmer who created this particular room; it is stored in the MUD's database and it will be displayed to everyone who cares to "look" at that room.

look

```
Penthouse
A cool northern light filters through the three big windows
in the north wall, which on a clear day provide a
breathtaking view all the way down the neon blur of Hitachi
to the beach. A huge king-size bed occupies a good part of
the room, sitting under two of the windows. A duvet the size
of Texas lies in a crumpled heap on the bed, a bunch of
pillows piled up at the head-end. The deep windowsills above
the bed are filled with those little things you want to have
handy while lying in bed... books, smokes, a glass jug
filled with water, cookies, the tv remote, a vase with some
plastic tulips and more...
You see a King-size bed and a Gothix Cyberdeck Diagnostic
Toolkit. You can go north (n), east (e), and south (s).
The south swings open
Tôsama arrives from the south.
The south swings shut.
```

Eveline, by "looking" at the room she is in, learns that it is called the Penthouse and she "sees" what it looks like from the description. "Doors" or "entrances" are regularly denoted by the compass direction in which they lead. Here the door to the south swings open because the player behind the character named Tôsama entered the command "`open north`" (because the door that lies to Eveline's south is to Tôsama's north) and when it opened, he stepped through it by entering the command "`go north`." The messages of the door swinging open and shut and Tôsama "arriving" from the south are generated by the MUD-program to show the players what is happening and who is going where.

The "`look character's_name`" command will display the name and description of that character. The description of the character has been written by the player of that character and it is stored in the MUD's database, so that every player "looking" at that character will automatically "see" the same description.

look Tôsama

```
Tôsama
A mature, Japanese male. Short height, average weight, well-
conditioned. Black, short hair, and brown eyes. He has some
lines around his eyes.
Tôsama is wearing a dark blue suit, comfortable-looking, but
very business-like. He is standing very casually, and he
looks back at you, with a half-smile in his eyes. Tôsama's
dufflebag hangs from his left shoulder. He wears a pair of
tough ankle boots.
He is in excellent health.
Tôsama is holding a credstick.
```

The description of Tôsama is followed by two game related messages, namely that he is in excellent health and that he is holding a credstick. The health status of the character is primarily of importance in combat situations, but also allows other players to react to the physical appearance of the character, whether s/he is in excellent health or covered with nasty cuts and bruises. What a character is holding in hir hands of course is also part of hir physical appearance and again allows other players to react (or not) when a character enters holding a cyberdeck or maybe an Uzi.

The "`emote`" command and its more sophisticated sibling "`pose`" allow the player to enter an action for hir character, which will be displayed in the room that the character is in at the moment. Here the player behind Tôsama "emotes" raising his eyebrow.

```
Tôsama raises an eyebrow.
```

For Eveline to react I, the player, need to enter the command shown below in bold-italic face:

emote smiles and limps over to fall into Tôsama's arms.

```
Eveline smiles and limps over to fall into Tôsama's arms.
```

The `emote` command and its data is parsed by the MUD program and the resulting text "`Eveline smiles...`" is send to the screens of every player whose character is in the same room as my character. Tôsama's player reacts by emoting in turn, etc.

```
Tôsama swears, softly, in Japanese.
```

emote holds on to Tôsama's shoulders and kisses him sweetly.

```
Eveline holds on to Tôsama's shoulders and kisses him sweetly.
```

emote hobbles back towards the bed.

`Eveline hobbles back towards the bed.`

Eveline was in dire need of a pair of boots and Tôsama had brought them. Tôsama's player, by entering the command "`give boots to Eveline`" hands over the boots he's carrying to Eveline. The resulting line of text is a standard line, generated by the MUD-program for the "`give`" command. Every time a player gives another player object X, everybody present will thus see "Player A hands Player B object X."

`Tôsama hands you a pair of steel toed boots.`

emote accepts the boots with a gentle bow.

`Eveline accepts the boots with a gentle bow.`

Since there is no automagically generated message when receiving something, I emoted accepting the boots.

The "`say`" command will let the character say something to the other people present in that room. There are numerous other commands (such as the "`wear`" command for clothing), but along with the "`go`" command ("`go north`," or "`go kitchen`"), these are the basic commands to navigate and communicate in most MUDs.

`Tôsama says, "I hope they fit."`

say let's see then...

`You say, "let's see then..."`

wear boots

`Eveline sits down and slides on her steel toed boots, one at a time.`

The command "wear boots" results in Eveline putting on the boots. The message that tells everyone in the room so is part of the "description" of the boots that is stored in the MUD's database. Every character "wearing" those boots would thus see the same message of "sitting down and sliding the boots on, one at a time" with hir name prepended. "Wearing" the boots is thus not an "emote" and Eveline really puts on a pair of boots.

To summarize then, part of the text outputted to the player consists of text generated by the MUD-program. The description of the Penthouse is stored in the MUD database and every time a player looks at it, s/he will receive the same description on hir screen. When a player uses the command for opening a door, the program will display to all the players present in that room which door swings open. If the player steps through the door then this is shown to hir, while the other players present will receive a message that such-and-so entered or left the room through that door. The messages generated by the MUD-program for entering and leaving a room or giving another player some object are very important for the role-playing experience. They, in a rather sublimated way, denote all those everyday sensorial cues we, largely unconsciously, pick up on, but that nevertheless keep us informed of what is happening in our immediate surroundings. Another part of the text is also stored in the MUD database, but has been inputted by the players themselves. The player behind Tôsama created the description of his character and every other player looking at him will receive this description from the MUD database where it is stored. Yet another part of the text consists of the actions and 'speech' of the characters, but this part of the text will not be stored in the MUD's database. The players merely use the MUD-program to display their actions and speech to one another and when the text scrolls off of the screen, it is gone.

The above scene is a very small example of interaction taking place on a MUD and it doesn't offer much information on who the characters are and what their relationship to one another is. One can however imagine that with growing involvement complex situations and relationships can be played out. And it is this playing of one's character, over a longer period, with the intention of presenting a well-rounded and consistent personality, that is called role-playing (RP).

CHAPTER 2

Constructing Dialogue and Gender

Speaking of Text

> `DoughBoy clutches his head and screams THE VOICES MADE ME DO IT!`
> `DoughBoy glances around, twitching nervously.`
>
> —Doughboy, *Cybersphere*

> Any time saying can be put in quotes it becomes a signified, what is spoken of by whatever is outside the quotes as in "... it becomes a signified, what is spoken of by whatever is outside the quotes as in...," and "the spoken" becomes at once "the spoken of" and other than "the spoken of."
>
> —Stephen Tyler, *The Unspeakable*

Eveline's is one of the voices that tell the story. I hope that for the reader throughout this text different voices will speak, argue and agree with one another, creating in a sense a dialogue. A dialogue in which each voice, the reader's voice included, can present a particular point of view, to show its affiliations and rootedness in order to momentarily evoke "... a fantasy whole abducted from fragments..." (Tyler 1987: 202). A dialogue that mirrors theory in experience and vice versa. While I try to fragment the story, to let different voices speak, there is no real dialogue to be found in this text and Eveline's voice is not really her voice. She just speaks the words that I, the author slash role player, let her speak. And as Stephen Tyler notes,

> [d]ialogue rendered as text... is no longer dialogue, but a text masquerading as a dialogue, a mere monologue about a dialogue... (Tyler 1987: 66)

One of the most defining qualities of cyberspace[13] probably is that it is the only place where a true dialogue can be textual without becoming a monologue. The text that remains after the typing is done may be static, nevertheless one of the qualities of text in real-time CMC is that it seems suspended, the durability and reliability of the words only lasting as long as they haven't scrolled off of the screen. Admittedly, the words that make up a "virtual text-based world" are quite a bit more solid than the ephemeral spoken word, but they are also quite a bit more fluid than the printed word. This text thus only reminds the reader of the dialogues that preceded the writing of this text. Still, even without a true dialogue *in* the text, I hope to remind the reader of the multitude of voices that make up life in a virtual world.

The voices that 'speak' throughout this text also play another role. While most everybody will have experienced the feeling of speaking differently, on another level, in different social situations, taking part in an online role-playing game is much more than just playing your part, speaking for your character. It is rather a delicate art of keeping track of shifting frames of reference and speaking in the right voice at the right moment in the right place. At any one moment a player can be involved in multiple simultaneous conversations that all take place on different levels, requiring the player to speak and act on various different levels at the same time. The two most obvious levels one can occupy are *In Character* (IC) and *Out Of Character* (OOC). The help files from Cybersphere explain the difference this way:

```
Showing verb help on '@ic':
----
Some actions taken on the MOO should be taken as yours--the
person typing the commands.  Others should be taken as your
character--your representation in the virtual reality.
You can make it clear to those around just _who_ you are by
using the @ic and @ooc commands.
@ic -- Go 'in character', playing your character.
@ooc -- Go 'out of character', being you.

Adding a ! to the command (@ic!, @ooc!) has one of two
effects:

If you are not already in the mode associated with the
command, you will be switched into that mode and those
around you will be informed.[14]
If you _are_ in that mode, the room will be reminded.  This
is useful if, for instance, your character is being
especially cruel and you want to remind everyone that it is
not YOU who are strangling that kitten, but
Sadistic_Kitten_Strangler.
```

It seems that when arguments arise, it is often about whether something is "good role-playing" or not, and whether a particular action must be classified as In Character or that the player in question acted impropriately, the action hence being classified as Out Of Character. The ideal of the role-playing game is to play one's character in another world, but for social and organizational reasons players also talk to each other *as themselves,* as the flesh and blood players behind the keyboard. In order to maintain a certain level of immersion in the virtual world at the level of the character, there are several commands and practices the players employ to distinguish between *In Character* interactions between the characters and *Out Of Character* interactions on the meta-level of the players. By using the `@ooc` and `@ic` commands the players can switch on and off an (OOC) flag appended to their name, signaling to all around that this character's player is currently only interacting as hirself and not as hir character. By using the `ooc` command (without the preceding @-sign) players can `say` or `emote` something OOCly, while their character remains IC.

Making use of these different modes of presence one can be speaking to a character in the same room ICly while speaking through *pages* with another player OOCly. Paging is a form of 'instant' communication, comparable to sending text messages with a cellphone, where one player can send a message to another player, whose character isn't necessarily present in the same room. Although IC and OOC are the two main categories for interaction in the MUD, within these two modes one can speak on a lot of different levels. Speaking or paging OOCly often serves to prepare or comment on a planned or ongoing RP situation. While the OOC mode of speaking is also used for correcting the most glaring spelling mistakes, one can often find players chatting OOCly about where they are from, how the weather is and how their day was. At the same time one can be involved ICly in a RP situation that requires that the character speaks with several people in the same room, while also keeping several IC conversations going through pages. As if this weren't enough the player can choose to play on several MUDs at the same time, actually playing several different characters at the same time. Or, in another window, the player could be reading and writing e-mail, designing web pages or writing on his thesis.

It is of this layering, these fuzzy boundaries and the slippage that occurs between them that the different voices speak. In a sense the text speaks with a forked tongue, on the one hand scientific prose leading the reader on, keeping hir on the narrow path of reason, while on the other hand the novelistic prose might force the reader to stop, consider and reconsider the point of view taken and reflect on the theory. Or maybe the novelistic prose insidiously tempts the reader to stray from the straight path of reason, skipping quickly through the scientific sections to the next part of the story. Or perhaps the novelistic paragraphs are merely tasty interjections in a larger theoretical tale. And who said that these different voices actually agree? At least those who speak will be heard, but only by those who choose to listen.

It is through the different modes of IC and OOC presence that I have conducted my work as an anthropologist in the city of New Carthage. The usual *modus operandi* of the anthropologist is participant observation and it involves the anthropologist accompanying the 'locals' during their daily or nocturnal activities for a prolonged period of time. The observations made during that time are usually complemented by information gathered through informal conversations and more formal, in-depth interviews. My participation in my informants' world went a bit further than the usual accompaniment during fieldwork. In order to truly enter New Carthage I had to "go native," I had to assume a character, I had to *be* a character, just to be able to walk around there. I felt I couldn't play an anthropologist as a character, because I didn't know how to fit an Anthropologist or a Researcher into the theme of the world. The awkward combination of IC and OOC qualities of such a character would probably interfere in an unacceptable way with the role-playing of other characters, let alone the problems it would create for role-playing that character myself. Such a character quite possibly would not have lasted more than a few days before it would be killed off as an annoying interference to the game. So when I first entered New Carthage, after playing a male character on another virtual world for a few months, I thought I might as well try out playing a cross-gender character myself and I created a female character named Eveline. At that point I was just another player and for a while I simply played my character, trying to get my bearings in this new world. I didn't expect this character to last more than a few weeks before she would be killed, but it would give me some insights into what it was like to be playing a cross-gender character, or so I reasoned. Apparently I must have done something right, because Eveline managed to survive for over three years and she and I grew from relative "newbies" to relative "oldbies."[15] After I announced that I was also doing research I didn't notice any major differences in the way Eveline was approached by other characters, apart from the occasional OOC question about how the research was going.

The material that I have collected differs from the normal fieldnotes and interviews in that everything I or Eveline has seen, done or said always already was text. Through the *log* function of the MUD client every word that ever appeared on my screen has been saved to the harddisk of my computer.[16] When discussing fieldwork in cyberspace, Sandy Stone notes that

> [i]n a universe in which everything (and everybody) is produced and mediated by text, the floppy disk is the ultimate field recorder. Nothing escapes its panoptic gaze. (1995: 243)

By making use of a text-indexing program I can quickly retrieve every conversation and every description verbatim. So not only do I have verbatim accounts of interviews, virtually everything that has happened in my or Eveline's presence during the research has been logged. My observations are purely textual and I haven't met any of my informants face to face. While this poses some unorthodox problems, I believe that one learns to speak and listen, or rather write and read in this world just as one would in a particular physical locale. After a while one starts to discern what kind of conversation one is having, which clues to pick up on and when informants are reluctant to speak about a certain subject. When the discourse has been incorporated it becomes easier to judge when a long silence is meaningful or if the person you're speaking with has simply stepped away from the computer to get some coffee. I have, however, tried to check my data with other players and against the information gathered from interviews and the questionnaire wherever possible.

The logs and other texts I have gathered are the result of my inquiry into a completely textual world as well as a result of my co-creating, co-propagating this world. One of the most important consequences of Geertz' influential article *Notes on the Balinese Cockfight* (1973) was the metaphorical liking of culture to text, or rather, in Geertz' own words,

> [t]he culture of a people is an ensemble of texts, themselves ensembles, which the anthropologist strains to read over the shoulders of those to whom they properly belong. (1973: 452)

Whereas Geertz is bound by the very fact that he uses a metaphor to express his way of making sense of culture, I am here regarding a whole world, metaphorically speaking, that is literally a text, or better, "textual." When I try to read these ensembles of text as Geertz suggests, I am really reading them. What I try to read however is not the text itself, but just like Geertz I try to understand the cultural mechanisms that animate this world. I am reading the participants' discourse in order to learn about how they create and operate a role-playing character of a particular gender.

My reading of this particular con/text however, is at the same time also a writing of it. Literally I am writing myself, my character into a virtual world and in a more metaphorical sense I am also writing its culture, partaking in the creation and continuation of its *mores.* The same goes for this scientific writing. While I try to make sense of this virtual realm ethnographically and anthropologically, I also write, create and continue several discourses, most notably those on "Role-Playing," "the Internet," "the Body," and "the Real and the Virtual." Anne Balsamo puts it very succinctly when she writes that

> [a]ny given text within a discursive system is a symbolic enactment of the cultural preoccupations of a particular historical conjunction. The relation of texts to one another is dialectical in that the intelligibility of any isolated work or text is always dependent upon the discourse within which it "makes sense" at the same time that the text in part constructs that very discourse. (Balsamo 1996: 4)

The material that I have collected can roughly be divided into two categories. Firstly there is the material that I have collected through "participant observation." Everything I have experienced or noted while I was role-playing my character, while I was IC, would fall in this category. The bulk of this material are the daily IC interactions between Eveline and other characters, but it also includes IC conversations on matters such as gender. I also have collected quite a bit of material from *lurking* in crowded rooms. It is a fairly common thing for characters to suddenly go silent or for players to announce they have to go Away From Keyboard (AFK). The character is then merely present as a dummy and is usually completely ignored until this character's player announces s/he's back at the keyboard. This situation of course offers the anthropologist a unique vantage point for unobtrusive observation.

Secondly, there is the material that I have collected through interviews, a questionnaire, and the examination of various websites. All this material results from OOC interactions and investigations. I chose to do "open" interviews and while I did have a prepared list of questions and topics for conversation, I usually based my interviews on a response to the questionnaire, a role-playing situation I and the informant had shared, or something s/he had remarked on OOCly, and then I would take the interview from there.

The questionnaire consisted of twenty questions, some closed, some open. I distributed the questionnaire in relevant newsgroups (the alt.rec.games.mud.* hierarchy) and I announced it on Cybersphere. I received a total of 68 replies, 26 (38%) from Cybersphere players and 42 (62%) from players of other MUDs who had reacted to my message in the newsgroups. From the total of 68 players 20 (30%) reported to be female, 47 (69%) male, and 1 player (1%) indicated to be of an other gender IRL. The mean age for the female players is 26.4 years (min=17, max=40) and 22.6 years (min=15, max=39) for the male players. Of the 26 Cybersphere players 7 (27%) reported to be female IRL and 19 (73%) male. The mean age for the female Cybersphere players is 21.2 years (min=18, max=27) and 20.2 years (min=15, max=29) for the male Cybersphere players. Kingfox, one of the wizards of Cybersphere, estimates that "`[c]ounting bits and their alts, we've got 331 player slots. But you figure there's some inactive people, and some bits who have characters. So I think 250-260 is a better guess at a semi-active userbase.`"

I also gathered (mostly background) information from websites dealing with role-playing. There are several "e-zines" about role-playing and quite a few websites that are dedicated to the more (or less) scientific study of CMC and MUDs. I visited quite a few homepages of players from Cybersphere (and other MUDs) where they present their characters or themselves.

Performing Gender

```
The Examiner asks, "So you're "Eveline_Edz" -- is that right?"
You say, "yes"
The Examiner asks, "All right, Eveline_Edz. Now -- your gender?
Male, female, spivak, or neuter?"
You say, "female"
The Examiner takes a small hand mirror from his desk and sets it
on the desktop in front of you.
The Examiner says, "Now, Eveline_Edz, I want you to describe for
me what you see. Describe your face, your body, your look -- the
form you'll wear in your time in this world."
```

—The Examiner, *Cybersphere*

> The social construction of gender and the gender attribution process are a part of reality construction. No member is exempt, and this construction is the grounding for all scientific work on gender.
>
> —Kessler and McKenna, *Gender. An Ethnomethodological Approach*

The player playing hir character in a MUD (usually) tries to portray a credible, convincing person within the theme of that world, using the tools the MUD provides, hir imagination, and hir social and communicative skills. When the player chooses to play a male or female character, part of the performance is playing a credible and convincing man or woman. The performance of the character is text-only and because the players don't have unmediated access to each other's physical bodies, the player cannot rely on hir body to immediately and naturally establish hirself, and by extension hir character, as male or female. The performance thus in part depends on the player enacting credible and convincing male or female speech, character traits and behavior in order to establish hir character as a credible and convincing man or woman, as a credible and convincing *person*. Now suddenly the question looms large what a 'real' man or a 'real' woman is, what they speak and act like, what the right rules for the role are.

Feminism and gender studies have convincingly argued that neither gender itself nor the roles attached to the different genders are set in stone. Early investigations, as for instance Margaret Mead's study *Sex and temperament in three primitive societies* (1935), showed that gender roles differ between different societies and different cultures. In some cultures for example, it is considered normal that men are caring and nurturing and that women are aggressive and prone to fighting, while these roles are by and large inverted in the West. Findings like these have functioned in various ways as therapeutic images for Western society, but the crucial fact that there are indeed biologically differing women and men wasn't challenged by these studies. What *was* established though, was the fact that gender became understood as the social or cultural expression of the biological sex. Indeed, these studies needed there to be two different genders in order to be able to show the arbitrariness of the gender roles.

Gender can seem very straightforward when it is defined as the cultural expression, the social construction of the natural, biological dichotomy of sex, female and male. When a child is born, we determine its gender and from that day on the child grows up as either a boy or a girl. Naturally we all seem know how to recognize a boy/man from a girl/woman, so in the normal everyday world there will be no major problems with acting and communicating appropriately to our respective genders. In gender studies the very naturalness of there just being two mutually exclusive genders is questioned and it turns out that even the "natural," "biological" dichotomy of two sexes, female and male, isn't as natural and clear cut as we might think. If one takes away the naturalness of gender this opens up the possibility of imagining gender not as expressive of some natural or biological identity, but rather as constituted in and through the performance of various gender acts. This construction of gender as performative is what Judith Butler argues for when she states that,

> [g]ender is in no way a stable identity or locus of agency from which various acts proceed; rather, it is an identity tenuously constituted in time – an identity instituted through a *stylized repetition of acts.* (Butler 1990: 270, italics in original)

While the discovery of the "sex chromosomes" was thought to be a unique and definite indicator of someone's sex, the sex chromosomes turned out to be less definite indicators than originally had seemed the case. When you are born, and lately often even before you are born, your sex[17] is determined and of course you're either a man or a woman, because you had a penis or a vagina. In those cases where the genitals don't provide a clear answer right away, other ways are available to determine the newborn's sex: most commonly a chromosome test, if the baby has an XX chromosome pair it's a girl, if it's got an XY chromosome pair it's a boy. But even the chromosomes, often deemed to be the defining principle of the human constitution, will not always act in a clearly dichotomous way. There are people with XXX, XXY, XYY and XO[18] chromosome 'pair' combinations and even within one individual a mix of for example XO and XXY cells can exist (cf. Kessler and McKenna 1978: 51-52; Birke 1992: 82, n.2). The unusual chromosomatic make-up of these people will not even always be noted since in a lot of cases these individuals will develop within society's standards as a woman or a man. Few, for instance, would mistake actress Jamie Lee Curtis for a man, although she has the chromosomatic (XY) make-up of a man.[19]

One would expect these facts to pose a question to the naturalness of the gender dichotomy, but usually these cases are dismissed as biological errors, which, in a sense, is understandable because the majority of people is born with clearly discernable genitals and an XX or XY chromosome make-up. Your biological make-up determines whether you're a woman or a man, the exception only proves the rule. There are however quite a few exceptions to that rule. Estimates put the percentage of people not conforming to the anatomical, endocrinological or genetic definitions of the male or female sex between 1.7 and 4 percent of the total population (Spaink 1998: 25). For every million children born that means that there are 4 Siamese twins, 1000 babies with Down syndrome, 1400 with a harelip and, at a conservative 1.7 percent, 17,000 with a genetic make-up that by medical definitions would make them not male, nor female (Spaink 1998: 28). The cultural imperative that there are two and only two mutually exclusive genders, male and female, is so strong that all those people don't figure in our everyday, common sense experience of the world. Even in science these bodies are dismissed as biological mistakes or relegated to a distant discourse such as gender studies, leaving the scientific mind unencumbered by the questions they pose to the popular conceptions of reality.

Transsexuals are yet another group of people proving the biological deterministic rule of sex wrong, as is the case of an XX woman getting a sex change surgery because "she" actually was a "he" born in the wrong body. Based on a psychological assessment of this individual's gender identity the decision can be reached by a medical gender team to perform a sex change surgery to adapt the individual's biological body to comply more satisfactory with her/his essential self. This medical practice of course conflicts with the idea that an individual's biological sex naturally determines whether s/he is a man or a woman. Contributing the origin, the determining focus point of a person's gender in one case to biological 'facts' and in the other to an essential self, gender identity seems indeed paradoxical. The conclusion must be that not only is "gender" a social construction, "sex" is so too. Sex and gender are the cultural fictions that organize our everyday, common sense reality and even science by and large succumbs to this particular reality fantasy. Kessler and McKenna, throughout their book, point out how, when and with what consequences the gender dichotomy[20] is constructed and place their argument in the wider context of constructionism, contending that,

> [i]n seeing the biological sciences as the foundation for all behaviours, we tend to overlook the fact that this is only one of an infinite number of ways of seeing the world. This does not mean, of course, that reality should or should not be constructed in this way; it only means that it is important to be aware that it is constructed. (1978: 42)

There are, however, also very important political consequences to th
truction of gender and even the deconstruction of science as the ulti
about the world. When one shows that gender and sex are not a natu
logical fact, but that they are social constructions, this opens up the possibility of considering the social, political and sometimes physical consequences that these constructions have for individuals. Constructing gender as a social construction also opens up the possibility of changing that construction, especially when this construction arises from the performance of gender by individuals.

According to Butler the performance of gender is organized in, on, around and through the body. This body of performance is not some sort of essential body; it is not a natural or biological body. The body and the suggestion of its facticity are the outcome of the very performance of that body. The appearance of a solid and continuous gender identity is installed through the performance of gender and that "discontinuous, stylized repetition of acts" installs those ideas as continuous, natural or biological truths. The fragmentary performance of the gendered body thus creates the illusion of continuity of a particular, gendered, biological body. This body is a social body, one that is only meaningful within the consensual framework that summons it up. Even though the meaningful body is socially constructed, Butler does not deny that body's materiality:

> [T]he existence and facticity of the material or natural dimensions of the body are not denied, but reconceived as distinct from the process by which the body comes to bear cultural meanings. (Butler 1990: 271)

The body *an sich* is not to be questioned here, but rather the process and the consequences of "gendering" and thus the construction of gender and gendered bodies should be questioned. It is important to note that even when the material facticity of the body is not questioned, this by no means constitutes a vote in favor of a biological or natural 'explanation' of gender. Rather than seeking refuge in a seemingly steadfast discourse, one should remember that,

> [m]eaning cannot (and does not wish to) change physical, material, and other phenomena; it itself is stronger than any force, it changes the total contextual meaning of an event and reality without changing its actual (existential) composition one iota; everything remains as it was but it acquires a completely different contextual meaning (the semantic transformation of existence). (Bakhtin in Schultz 1990: 141)

However, before we ask what the consequences of a particular, contextual meaning are, we should consider the processes by which that meaning was created. In the case of gender we should look into how a body becomes a gendered body in order to learn about the processes at work.

Butler accomplishes two important things with her rendering of gender as performative. Firstly, she deconstructs the internal continuity and the appearance of substantiality of gender identity and secondly, she puts the performing body on stage, in ethnomethodological brackets as it were, for us to inspect its act. This gender-act takes quite literally the form of a stage play when Butler says that a meaningful body "...is fundamentally dramatic" (1990: 272).

> By dramatic I mean only that the body is not merely matter but a continual and incessant *materializing* of possibilities. One is not simply a body, but, in some very key sense, one does one's body and, indeed, one does one's body differently from one's contemporaries and from one's embodied predecessors and successors as well. (Butler 1990: 272)

It is easy to dramatize this point of view and say that "all the world is a stage." Indeed, making the performance of gender larger than life by putting it on stage runs the risk of someone pointing to the analysis of a certain gender-act and, as in the theatre, saying "This is just an act" (cf. Butler 1990: 278). This de-realizing and bracketing of a gender-act as an act allows the spectator to stick to hir common sense beliefs, even when faced with their very constructedness. *This* particular gender act is de-coupled from actual reality and framed as an act, and by placing it outside of everyday reality, by the very fact that a certain behavior is named a gender *act*, it exempts the spectator from questioning hir everyday beliefs.

In common sense, everyday situations the natural, continuous appearance of gender still holds true. Or, as Butler puts it,

> [t]he tacit collective agreement to perform, produce, and sustain discrete and polar genders as cultural fictions is obscured by the credibility of its own production. The authors of gender become entranced by their own fictions whereby the construction compels one's belief in its necessity and naturalness. (1990: 273)

Even though the everyday reality of gender is very resilient, the framing of gender as performative allows the researcher to study how in fact the gender-act is performed. Butler says that,

> [g]ender is instituted through the stylization of the body and, hence, must be understood as the mundane way in which bodily gestures, movements, and enactments of various kinds constitute the illusion of an abiding gendered self. (1990: 270)

Butler thus frames reality and by analyzing the various mundane, common sense enactments of gender we can start to understand how these particular, discontinuous acts form the continuous, dichotomous, and largely heterosexual backdrop for our lives.

It is in online role-playing games that we are offered a particularly interesting view of the mundane and common sense ways that gender is constructed. A player will construct a character as s/he sees fit and will try to play this character as s/he believes this character would have acted in the particular circumstances. The player consciously constructs the character, its gender, its appearances, its actions and its motivations. Literally everything that makes up the character or that occurs has to be typed out. In order to create a meaningful character the player has to make use of social conventions, imagery and ways of communication that are already in place in the larger whole of Western society.[21] The player, after all, is not operating in a vacuum, but is trying to role-play with other players who must be able to make sense of the actions of each other's characters. The player may be aware of the implications and effects of some of those social conventions, images and ways of communication, but since this player shares the Western mindset s/he can't question every last detail of them all the time. In order to role-play s/he has to rely on mundane enactments and common sense performances to get hir message across.

It became clear early in my research that whatever the gender-configuration of a certain player-character duo was,[22] most players are primarily concerned with the most salient character traits and psychological motivations of their character, rather than with gender *an sich*. While of course a man would act differently than a woman, these differences don't seem to faze most players when they're role-playing, not even when they're role-playing a cross-gender character. Usually, it is stated, it is much more important whether the character is aggressive or not, really talkative or more silent, prone to engage in a relationship or more of keeping a personal distance, etc. These character traits are closely linked to the kind of role the character is playing; is the character a mercenary, a pilot, a fixer, a medical doctor, an employee of a corporation, or a reporter? These are some of the more well-known archetypes (in Cyberpunk RPGs), but the options and variations are basically limitless. This creates a situation very similar to how people 'handle' gender IRL. The gender of the character mostly informs the role-playing of that character implicitly. In certain situations the player might be particularly conscious of the gender of hir character, just as IRL, and act accordingly, but usually gender does not play a particularly conscious role in the role-playing of the character even though it still informs that role-playing.

In the following sections I will consider various sites of mundane and common sense enactments of gender in an online role-playing game. I will especially focus on the ideas, conventions and practices of naming, describing and role-playing a character. Although it might seem that by setting apart and analyzing these particular aspects of gender and MUDs they become divorced from our everyday, common sense world, they really are embedded in a larger whole, not only that of a particular online RPG, but also that of the "West".

> Members [of a particular culture] do not simply learn rules for telling females from males. They learn how to use the rules in their relation to the socially shared world of two genders. There is no rule for deciding "male" or

> "female" that will always work. Members need to know, for example, when to disregard eyebrows and look for hand size. Gender attributions are made within a particular social context and in relation to all the routine features of everyday life... (Kessler and McKenna 1978: 158)

While players who interact with others through their characters are not confronted with actual, physical bodies, a whole arsenal of techniques and "virtual bodies" makes up for the lack of materiality. Indeed, it may be the case that materiality itself starts to take on new meanings in the realm of the virtual.

A Swish of Lace

Eveline [to Lillith]: If she was going to what? To die and I could choose to die with her?

Lillith leans forward, grey eyes beginning to sparkle with interest. She nods slightly.

Lillith [to Eveline]: Right. If you could choose.

Eveline closes her eyes for a moment, lips tightening as she thinks and then leans towards Lillith, placing her elbows on the table, "I would... more for me even than for her to be honest. I've seen too many of my friends and lovers die... Last night I crawled into my coffin with a shitload of sleepers, but I still woke up... I'm still comfortably numb you know..."

Lillith leans back all the way, resting her back against the booth and closing her eyes. She places a hand on her chest and sighs, "That's _perfect_. Beautiful."

Lillith eventually opens her eyes to look at you.

Eveline leans back as well and looks at Lillith quizzically.

Lillith [to Eveline]: Tell me you're an artist.

Eveline blinks and looks at her fingers, then back up at Lillith, "I never think about myself as an artist, but I play the bass... used to play in a slash-n-burn band... not quite what you'd call artistic..."

Lillith leans forward again, swiftly at first, but slowing as she catches herself. "Yes. But don't you feel the need to create? To slap a city of drunken assholes awake and tell them how pathetically beautiful they are, at least to you?"

Eveline sings softly, hoarsely, a bluesy tune, "Beautiful people... you ride the same subway as I do... eveeeeery mooorning..."

Eveline smiles to Lillith, hiding real emotion.

Lillith closes her eyes again, and says in the loudest voice you've heard thus far, "_Finally_."

Eveline [to Lillith]: Finally what...?

Lillith sings in a whispering croon, "Sometimes I dream.. while all the other people dance.. sometimes I dream of Charlotte Sometimes."

Eveline looks at Lillith with a face of wonderment and admiration and nods, more to herself than to Lillith, "Quite a voice..."

Lillith slides out of the booth.

Eveline turns on the bench to look at Lillith standing and raises an eyebrow, questioningly.

Lillith circles around the booth with a swish of lace, her steps those of one possessed or climbing a slight incline, and stands behind you, lowering her head to your shoulder.

Lillith whispers, "Would it be more tragic to paint you surrounded by the living or the dead?"

Eveline breathes quickly and shallowly and lets her chin drop to her chest, the side of her head resting gently against Lillith's head, "The living are always more tragic than the dead... Painting me among the dead would mean consolation to me, it's among the living that I'm wandering, grasping... waiting."

Lillith whispers, "Do you find me childish? Immature?"

Eveline whispers, "If anything... you seem true to me" to Lillith.

Lillith circles with a dancer's speed back to her side of the booth.

Lillith slides into the booth.

Eveline raises her head and her gaze slowly, breathing more slowly again.

Lillith clasps her hands on the table before her. "You find my inexperience unattractive?"

Eveline wraps one arm over her belly, hand in her side, the other resting on the table and looks at Lillith, "Inexperience in what?"

Eveline grins slightly, "So far... you seem to play me very well..."

Lillith dips her head down slightly, staring at you from the tops of heavily-painted eyes. "My life is made of nothing more than movies, books, and music. I'm not a proper child of the world. Didn't you.. smell it?"

Eveline nods pensively and winks at Lillith cheekishly, "Cherish that... for as long as you can. And yes, I... smelled it as you say, but it charms me... It's a little like remembering the days of the Black Angels... The rush of the new, the being on top of it all... I try to savour the image you present me, with all your knowledge of a world that seems a little better from every angle..."

CHAPTER 3

In the Sphere

Names

> `Lillith says, "I will give you a secret. My birth name is Marianne. Keep it."`
> `Eveline nods again, a stunned look on her face, "i will keep it... keep it close to my heart and no one will know..."`
>
> —Lillith & Eveline, *Cybersphere*

> The name of the self is not an "auto-nomy"; it is the name spoken antinomously by an other. It is the emicant [ay] of the emanent other.
>
> —Stephen Tyler, *The Unspeakable*

The character's name is the first thing you see about a character you haven't met before. The name is the first impression and should ideally be an indication of the type of person the character is, or as one player put it: "`[The name] should be accurate, concise and give the viewer a good overall picture of what to expect.`" Names are usually chosen from a wide array of real and 'fictional' names. With fictional names I mean those names that are derived from mythology, literature, pop music, TV shows or movies. These kind of names are not usually used IRL; few people are called Thor, Zeus, Shakespeare, Abbalover, Alf or Braveheart IRL. Some names taken from the above sources are of course names that are also used IRL, such as Jesus, Eric, Case, Mulder, etc. Nouns, adjectives and verbs are also chosen as a character names, usually on grounds of their connotative or associative meanings. For example Nightmare, Rattler, Spooky and Shining. Curtis notes that

> [o]ne can pick out a few common styles for names (e.g., names from or inspired by myth, fantasy, or other literature, common names from real life, names of concepts, animals, and everyday objects that have representative connotations, etc.), but it is clear that no such category includes a majority of the names. (1992: 353)

While Curtis' observation might be valid for most social MUDs, on role-playing MUDs actual names from the real and the fictional categories seem to make up the biggest part of the characters' names. When we regard the reasons players state for choosing a particular name for their character it becomes more apparent that there is a difference between social MUDs, where one could be said to 'play' a persona, and role-playing MUDs, where one is supposed to play a character.

On the surface the difference between a "persona" and a "character" may not seem very great, but there is quite a fundamental difference between the two. A persona is an extension of the player behind it, a projection, however partially or warped, of the person behind the keyboard. The persona, taking into account all the distancing and transformational effects of cyberspace, in a key sense represents the player hirself and as such the player is ultimately accountable for what the persona says or does. On the other hand, the character is generally (or ideally) seen as a creation of the player, much like a character in a book or a movie. Like in a book or a movie the player will have to be close to the character to be able to portray it convincingly, but the player will ideally not be held responsible for what hir character says or does *In Character*, because the character is just that: a character. This last clause is a very important one, because what the character says or does, must fall within the perimeters of what is generally considered "good role-playing" in order to exempt the player from ultimate accountability. The character for instance can kill, rob or cheat another character and if the player makes sure that this all happens within the limits of good role-playing, then the player will not be held accountable for the actions of the character; the character however might have to face some IC repercussions.

The line between a persona and a character can seem very thin, especially because the name of the character functions as an identifier on several different levels. On one level (In Character) it points to the character as a character, while on another level (Out Of Character) it points to the player behind it. It is here that in effect the name of the character functions as the name for the player's persona, or the player hirself. Tôsama, one of the characters I interacted with a lot, is a university professor aged forty IRL. His character is a Japanese 'businessman' roughly his own age, which makes Tôsama both one of the oldest players and one of the oldest characters on Cybersphere. IC Tôsama is a very reserved man, verging on the mysterious, who nevertheless is very sociable. Tôsama just never really speaks much about himself. OOC Tôsama turned out to be a perceptive and thoughtful observer, who remarked the following about the differences between a persona and a character:

```
For RPG, the name is even more important, since it is the
first thing learned, generally. It sets the tone for the
character, and creates a cue for observers' expectations.
So, choosing a name is the same as 'making a first
impression'. Generally, they're lasting. [...] For MOOing
```

> in general, I think the name becomes even more personal, initially. One becomes attached to one's character, and is conscious of the impressions one creates, even 'behind the mask'. Hence, the tendency of (on a social moo) persons (controllers) with established characters, to use 'guests' to behave in ways they wouldn't want associated with their usual 'self' characters.

Tôsama refers to both a character and a persona as "character", but he tries to clarify the same distinction I just made between a persona and a character. A name that is like making a first impression applies to the character; setting the tone and creating a cue for the observers' expectations is something that the player consciously tries to create for hir character. The first impression a name creates in "MOOing in general" shows the thin line between a character and a persona: the name becomes more personal, the player becomes more attached to the character and becomes more conscious of the impressions that s/he makes, even if it is "behind the mask". What was initially 'just' the name of the character has now taken on some of the qualities of the persona and hence also refers more directly to the player. When Tôsama refers to "social MOOs" the "established" and "self" characters refer to what I call the persona. Because the persona is how the player usually presents hirself on a social MUD, the player will employ more or less anonymous guest characters to avoid getting a bad name. The distinction between character, persona and player is not absolute, but rather a question of keeping track of the appropriate frame of reference.

Players in general agree on the importance of choosing a name, although a few remarked that any name would do, as long as it is "cool." "[Y]ou basically just name your character after a cool guy you saw in a movie once, or something," one player simply stated. The names of the players who "just" choose a cool name don't differ remarkably from the names of the players who place particular importance on choosing the "right" name. The reason for this might be that most players seem to pick a name from the same broad categories of real and fictional (nick)names for human characters. A few players said that they didn't pay any extra attention to the names of characters they encountered. One player said: "I view a character's name mostly the same as I view it in real life, I can read into it whatever I want, but I still have to see the character in action before I can make a judgement about them." Another player said that she mainly focused on the description of the character, rather than the name, because she considers the description to carry more information about the character than the name. I will turn to the descriptions and the role-playing itself in the next sections, as these are also important for the "reading" of a character.

Liking a name is important to most players; it has to have a certain ring or interesting connotation for the player. Graye remarked that it is hard to form an attachment to a character with a very generic name, such as "Bob," because it doesn't convey an evocative image and therefore it would be difficult to write a description for the character. Another player noted that a character with a realistic, but original and creative name means that the player is serious about the character and will probably be interested in role-playing. This orientation stands in contrast to players who choose a "stupid," or "bullshit" name for their character, such as "Deathbringer," "Nightstalker," "Twit" or "PhUkU666." While the first two of these names can under circumstances function as a legitimate nickname for a character, most players agree on the fact that these names indicate that the player is quite possibly not interested in serious role-playing, but rather that they're after "winning" the game. Names like these are commonly associated with cheating (abuse of MUD-code), obnoxious behavior and random killing of other characters. Players indulging in such behavior are often referred to as "twinks."

The original context and connotations of the names players choose play an important part in the construction of the character. The name and what is variously termed as "a core identity", "style" or "image" of a certain (fictional) person are used to build one's own character on. One player said that she took the whole concept of a movie character and had made her own character in its image, taking the movie character's name, appearance, "style" and history, because she liked it so much. Some players however construct their characters by starting out with an idea of a "core identity" for their characters and then search for a fitting name. Others use a name because it fits the ethnic background of the character or because they think it particularly fits the gender of their character.

Some players note that the ethnic or gender specificity of a name also works the other way around, viz. when someone associates a particular name with a certain gender or ethnic background they will often approach a character as if it really is of that gender or ethnic background. When I asked a player about why a female character did use a male name, I was told that this particular name was actually a female name in Arabic. Another player noted about this character that it detracts from the RP that upon encountering a character with a "male" name one learns that the character is female. The same player however told me that her own character had no "real" name (i.e. a proper first and last name) but only a more or less gender-neutral nickname. She said that the fact that her character does not have a real name did contribute to the RP and in fact was one of the most defining characteristics of her character.

One player showed the relative merits of a just name or just a name by saying: "`Making an incredibly good name and then getting offed`[23] `casu-`

ally is upsetting. I do not know if [the name is] really important. Just more data. More conversation fuel." By the same token that discounts the importance of a character's name, this player makes it into a very important aspect of the character. While a name is "just more data," it is also a starting point for a conversation that will lead to a mutual exchange of information about who these characters are and why they are named the way they are.

Several players noted that the character's name not only contains information about the character itself, but about the player of that character as well. Graye is a very vocal character/player who usually presents his opinion in long, but well versed and to the point statements. Playing his character on Cybersphere for approximately four years Graye is one of the longest living characters, even though he's only twenty-one IRL. Graye observed that a character's name largely reflects the OOC attitude of the player behind it. When read carefully, he said, one can determine whether the player plays the character for "amusement, silliness, RP [or] social activity in an OOC style." It is important to know to a certain extend what a player is up to with his or her character, in order to meaningfully assess the cues the player gives off and react properly. While a generic name like "Bob" does not give the player much IC information about what kind of person this character is, it can still be meaningfully read in an OOC way. Graye puts it like this:

> [W]ith more traditional names, a character's name is often simply arbitrary, and prevents predetermined insights or judgements into that character; that is, a character's name will be something like "William Johnson," and any conclusions about the character will have to be made through RP contact, not guesswork. It's interesting to note, however, that the name "William Johnson," does describe an OOC RP style; most people who'd choose a name like that tend to think more deeply into their character than somebody who chooses the name "Death," or "Rigor Mortis."

Learning to read and write the particular discourse of online role-playing games and the discourse developed on the particular virtual world one is participating in, is thus essential to successfully presenting a believable character with an appropriate name. This learning process is illustrated by Shadowschild who remarks that:

> Most role players that i have noticed choose a 'desc' name first [a "descriptive name", like for instance "Shadows-child"], from their histories of D&D or MUDs... then the character is killed off (sometimes deliberately) and they come back with a 'normal' name to play more seriously in the

```
RPing game. Some then revert, after 'diving wholeheartedly'
into the game and create a deeper character who has a
'cover' name... a history that requires or results in a
'desc' name instead of or in complement to a 'normal' name.
```

In one way or another virtually every player said that s/he tried to "read" the characters' names in a meaningful way. This of course is, in the context of a MUD, a sensible thing to do. Most players choose a name with care and deliberation, trying to make it something that enhances the image they wish to convey with their character. The name ideally must convey an image of what you can expect from this character and its player, mainly ICly, but also OOCly. The name of a character generally is read that way by the players in order to make sense of that character, in terms of gender, ethnicity, general disposition or "style" of the character and OOC player motivation. This means that the way a name is read, will largely determine how one's initial attitude towards that character and its player will be. As Tôsama noted about my character, Eveline:

```
For example, "Eveline", has connotations ... a somewhat
delicate female name. In that sense, the observer 'projects'
onto that player, the beliefs and affects connected with
"Eveline" in their stored schema. After time, as "Eveline"
is 'learned', the observer stores new information about
_this_ Eveline.
```

Thus a character is named, not by the player, but by other characters and the actual name of the character is merely a starting point. Maybe not merely a starting point, it is a very important departure, where the player, conforming to consensus and discourse, chooses an archetype. Working from this model, through the words and reactions of the player's 'opponents', the player grows the character, being only partly in control.

Descriptions

```
males say "blue" females say "aqua", "sapphire",and
"dark navy"
```

—Shadowschild, *Cybersphere*

Before you can read me you've gotta learn how to see me

—En Vogue, *Free your mind*

The description of a character is one of its most defining features. A name may convey a very general image and provide the player with a baseline for the character, still the control of the player over just what a name conveys is tenuous to say the least. The description of the character however offers a much more versatile and detailed way of crafting a convincing person from one's character and as with a character's name there are numerous ways of reading a description. Every character has a description that is written by its player and creating it is usually one of the very first things one does when entering a new MUD. The description is visible to everyone who is in the same room by using the "look" command. On Cybersphere and most other role-playing MUDs I have visited, the average description runs about eight to twenty lines in length. Of course there are exceptions where a description consists of merely a few words or, quite the opposite, runs well over a hundred lines. Both of these extreme cases are generally considered to detract from the playability of the game and are said to breach the suspension of disbelief.

In the case of a very short description it obviously offers other players rather little to act on. A description is, as it were, a character's virtual body and a three word description means that it is hard to form a mental image of that body, and thus of the character that it is meant to portray. This is detrimental to the interaction because even virtual bodies do gesticulate and move about in the virtual space they are in. Too short a description makes it hard to see the situation and the characters in it before the mind's eye.

In the case of a very long description there are two obvious problems. The first is that the description is so long that it will scroll off the screen. This means that if you want to read the whole description you will have to scroll back through the text. This is problematic because it forces the player to interact with the MUD-client, which doesn't do much good for the suspension of disbelief. The ideal is that the use of the MUD-client is so natural that it becomes transparent to the user when s/he's interacting with/in the MUD. The second problem is that reading a very long description takes too much time and the player can't partake in the simultaneously ongoing role-playing while catching up. Good descriptions are therefore often dense, finely crafted pieces of text punctuated with qualifiers. "`Description is important - Brief but elaborate! (if that _is_ possible :),`" as one player remarked.

In most MOOs[24] the description of the character is simply a piece of text, written by the player for the character, that is stored in the MOO's database. Cybersphere is slightly different from other MOOs in that it has a fully functional implementation of clothing. Often, from a software point of view, clothing doesn't exist as such; it is simply part of the description of the character. In Cybersphere however actual pieces of clothing can be purchased ready made or they can be fashioned from "blank" pieces of cloth by the players themselves. The clothing can be worn and taken off again; it can be sold or left on the couch. In a MOO everything that exists from a software point of view is an "object", a piece of code that has a set of features and belongs in the MOO's database. For instance an exit is an object and its features let a character "go through" it and it will then transport the character to the appropriate adjoining room. A room also is an object that can be "entered" through an entrance/exit and has a certain description. A character too is an object; one that is controlled by a player and naturally features a description. Different features on a character object allow the player to "speak" and "emote" through that character. When I say that on other MOOs clothing as such doesn't exist, I mean that there are no objects that represent pieces of clothing, the clothing that is there only exists as part of the description that is stored on the character object and can be called up by a player using the "look" command. In Cybersphere however clothing is made out of objects, which means that you can buy an object called "A pair of black pants" that has a feature that allows it to be "worn". When the pants object is worn by the character object it will modify the description stored on that character and the parts of the body defined by the @coverage of the pants-object will now show not the description of the character, but the description of the pants instead. Implementing clothing this way is a strain on the available database space and is therefore often forgone. However, being able to enter a room and actually take off your coat adds to the realism of the experience.

One of the consequences of there being actual pieces of clothing available in Cybersphere is that characters can also be naked. The complete description of a character thus consists of three different parts. The first part of the description is the standard description that all MOOs use. Since the clothing that the character wears is shown separately from this general description, the more or less implicit consensus in Cybersphere is that the first part of the description should be a very general overview of the character, height, build, posture and a few obvious traits. The second part of a character's description are the messages to be displayed for the naked body. These messages are broken down into small descriptions specific for the hands, feet, legs, arms, chest, abdomen, groin, neck and head. Clothing forms the third part of the description and for each piece of clothing one has to define which areas it covers. When a character wears clothing that, for example, leaves the abdomen uncovered, we might see that this character has a pudgy belly and a navel piercing. The clothing thus actually layers over the character's naked body, almost like it would IRL. Most players make a few unique pieces of clothing for their character in order to match the description of the clothing to the image that they want their character to convey. Below is the description of Lillith, the way she looked when Eveline first met her in an old coffeehouse, `where [a]n ancient neon sign in the window buzze[d] and crackle[d], attempting to spell out C-O-F-F-E-E.`

```
Lillith
You see a 5'8" female, about 18 or 19, poised on the brink of
  womanhood. Her dark black hair is cut boyishly short, long
  bangs hanging in soft feathery tufts around her eyes - pale,
  smoke-grey, flickering slightly with each change in her environ-
  ment. Her skin is a deathly pale white, and although rather
  slender, a well-proportioned figure suggests a graceful body.
Her face is powdered white, heavy black makeup on her eyes and
  lips accentuating her calm grey eyes. A small diamond stud
  glitters in her left nostril. Her long neck is slender and
  pale, her throat quavering slightly with each breath. A dark
  black crescent moon is tattooed just above her collarbone. A
  long black cloak, constructed of a thick silky material,
  secures at her chest with a silver rose-shaped clasp. Ruffles
  line the trim of the cloak, and a hood hangs off the shoulders.
  A small, bright silver pentacle rests at the base of her
  throat, held on a thin chain about her neck. Her hands are a
  soft white, each long finger ending in a nail painted a glossy
  black. Bright white scars criscross each wrist just below her
  palms. A long black skirt falls to her ankles. Made of a thin,
  gauzy lace, it is cut in a slight ripple, a pattern of roses
  embroidered across its surface. Thin, pale legs are faintly
  visible beneath the tissue material. A pair of antiquated black
  leather riding boots rise to her shins. They are high-heeled
  and are secured by means of four leather straps rising from
  ankles to knee, in the classic Victorian fashion.
She is in excellent health.
Lillith is empty-handed.
```

The first part of Lillith's description is the general part of the description that is featured on all MOOs. On other MOOs usually the description of the character's clothing is included here. The second part of the description, starting with "Her face is powdered...", is where in Cybersphere the MOO-program puts together the different descriptions of the naked body and the clothing that the character wears. Apparently Lillith doesn't wear anything that covers the face or the neck, because the description here shows details about them that would not be visible had she been wearing a scarf or a helmet for instance. The rest of her body is covered by different pieces of clothing, except for her hands and wrists. The description is complemented by two game related messages, namely that Lillith is in excellent health and that she's not holding anything in her hands.

Not all players put as much thought and care into their description as the player of Lillith. One evening, Eveline went downtown to Club XS to meet for business with one of the city's most feared crime lords, mr. simon aka the White Rabbit.

```
Pounding through the club, the deep thud of bass pulses through
   the floor and walls, sending the screaming beat of the music
   alive throughout the club. Lights flash and fade, lancing
   through the air as they strike and bedazzle, setting the
   entire eastern end of the club alight. Rising about five feet
   from the floor, a large stage runs out from the eastern end of
   the north wall. Figures spin and twist onstage, their flailing
   movements lost in the haze of light and sound. Pressed
   together, dancers cover the floor, a mass of faceless bodies
   vanishing in the throng. The western end of the club lies in
   almost total darkness, with only the occasional light piercing
   the shadows.
```

In the corner, speaking with mr. simon, stands a man Eveline has never seen before. One of simon's goons? A new 'business' affiliate? Wearily she inspects the stranger before approaching the two men at the far end of the bar.

```
Shepard
A bad dream
Shepard wears a well-fitting black, combat helmet. Strapped to
   Shepard left shoulder is a heavily oiled holster. He wears a
   thick gray overcoat, sleek and shiny like metal. Shepard is
   wearing skin tight white leather gloves. A heavy chrome buckle
   supports a thick black leather belt strapped around his waist,
   dangling from the belt a leather pistol holster gleams from
   beneath an oiled ebony surface. He wears a pair of tough steel
   toed boots.
He is in excellent health.
Shepard is holding a credstick.
```

Here we see that the general description merely says, "A bad dream." This very short and not very descriptive comment is slightly compensated by the fact that the clothing that Shepard wears is automatically shown in the description too.[25] For regular players however this doesn't add much detail to act on because all of Shepard's clothing is bought in a store and thus features well-known standard descriptions.

In order to successfully interact with other characters the players must continually read important information off of each other's characters. Especially with characters that one hasn't interacted with (much) yet, the description often offers important information about what one can expect from that character. Tôsama thinks that,

> Initially, while the character is becoming 'known' to the other players, [the description] is everything; over time decreasing in importance, as others see whether the player's game play is congruent with the description.

A player whose character's description read, "nothing," smiled ruefully at me and explained that it was his fourth character in a month. One can imagine the frustration of having one's character killed and having to come up with yet another name and description, especially when you have spend some serious effort on creating that character and the dying part occurs so often. Walking around as "nothing" for a while is thus understandable, but not very conducive to role-playing.

One of the first things I noticed was that virtually every description has pronounced gender markers in the first three lines. The player uses either words like "female" or "male" (see also Lillith's description) or, more implicitly, pronouns to refer to the character in hir description. Thinking there might be a difference between those descriptions explicitly using nouns to describe the character and those that featured pronouns, I started out with counting both types of descriptions.

From a period of about a year I have extracted 214 character descriptions from my logs. This collection is fairly random, the extracted descriptions being of the characters that I had met during that year and interacted with for long enough to "look" at them.[26] Of the total of 214 descriptions, 144 (67%) were of male characters, 62 (29%) of female characters, 6 (3%) of gender-neutral characters (5 neuters and 1 spivak) and 2 (1%) "other".[27] Of the 144 male descriptions 77 featured the word "male", "man", or "guy" and 67 featured a male pronoun in the first three lines. Of the 62 female descriptions 33 featured the word "female", "woman", "girl", or "lady" and 29 featured a female pronoun. So for both the female and the male descriptions 47% of the descriptions featured 'just' a pronoun and 53% featured a noun naming the character's gender. Apart from this bias towards using a noun as primary gender marker in the descriptions I couldn't find any other significant differences in the descriptions. In both the female and the male categories there were long and short descriptions, very elaborate and much more tersely phrased descriptions.

Interestingly all the gender-neutral (and the two "other") characters featured short descriptions, painting them as sickly or unsavory characters. They featured such malformations as massive scarring, pale and sickly demeanors, bright red, blue or "mustard yellow" colored eyes and/or grossly disfigured genital areas. I have not been able to obtain much more information about gender-neutral characters on Cybersphere. I met all these characters early in the research, when apart from logging my "travels" I had not properly begun conducting interviews. Apart from one player, who played two neuter characters for quite a while, the other characters did not live for very long; this player I regrettably did not get a chance to interview for various reasons. Another player, whose character description I have not been able to obtain, commented on his character in response to the questionnaire,

```
Playing a spivak on Cybersphere went down very well, I feel
that I played it successfully (until I was bored of the
character.) I had many people, annoyingly, asking what my
real sex was, as they supposedly couldn't pick it from my
role play style. It was fun, but quite a bit of work to keep
up.. it's that extra little piece of thinking before you say
or do anything that can get tiresome.. I think, maybe I
shall do it again someday.
```

Danet (1996: n.p.) reports that some 20 to 30 percent of the players chooses an unconventional gender, but my research does not show similar interests among the players of Cybersphere. While I have no supporting data on other role-playing MUDs, my impression is that this is because Cybersphere is a *role-playing* MOO, where the characters one plays much more resemble characters from a movie or a novel, as opposed to the less genre-bound "personae" that inhabit the social MUDs on which Danet reports. Cybersphere is thus by and large populated by female and male characters, assumedly played by female and male players, and the occasional references I make to gender neutral characters are largely based on literature and the general cultural knowledge that I have acquired as a role player. I believe that it would be safe to say that on Cybersphere "ungenderedness" isn't widely regarded as a very desirable avenue for role-playing.

When discussing descriptions OOCly or in an interview, players offered information on what makes a good description and what in particular makes a good female or male description. One of the things often noted, apart from the admonition to be "brief but elaborate", is that the description should offer a lively impression of that character without explicitly describing the effects of the description for the looker.

```
What I feel makes a good description is one that does not
impose perception upon the looker (i.e. 'You are scared just
by looking at this guy' is a bad one).. one that expresses a
degree of realism. As to what would pique my interest, it
```

would be a character whose emotions or personality were very visible in them physically.. in other words, an expressive character. Someone with a very visual personality [...] just like real life, someone with a posture, stride, and manner of speech that give clues to their identity. [T]hey don't have to be obvious...

Lillith's comment touches on a few important points one should consider when reading and writing a character's description. The first observation is that you shouldn't try to impose a certain perception upon the looker, something that Lillith elaborated on in a message to the BBS:[28]

I've composed a very short list of things included in people's [descriptions] that, (and I point out immediately that this is strictly my opinion and by no means a statement of definite fact) due to their repetitiveness and/or lack of creativity and/or use of very tired cliche's, are the sort of things that make me grumble/yawn/sigh upon seeing them. They are as follows: "He/She has wisdom beyond their years." It obviously isn't beyond their years if they have it, is it? "He/She has eyes that seem to pierce straight through you," or, if you prefer, "He/She has eyes that seem to look right into your soul." I'd sure hate to be in a room with two people piercing through each other with their eyes. That'd get messy, I think. "He/She radiates an aura of pure evil." Sorry, I can't think of anything witty about this. "Blah" is the only thing that seems to enter my head. "He/She is amazingly/ravishingly/arousingly/etc. beautiful/handsome." What if you're not my type? What if you're blonde, brunette, or whatever, and it (for some reason) is a major turn-off for me? People generally decide for themselves whether something is beautiful or ugly. Well, unless you watch too much tv. But that's another argument altogether. There are probably many others, but these really stick in my craw. I'm sorry if I'm directly offending anyone who might be reading this, but I think we're all capable of being a lot more original. Mainly, I just hate it when people decide for me in their [description] how I view them.

Perception and appreciation are highly individual processes and rather than trying to impose a certain understanding of the character upon the other player, one should try to make the description more like a novelistic characterization with particular traits and habits of the character appearing in the text.[29] The line here is a thin one: when are you imposing perception on the looker and when are you still acceptably characterizing? "Eyes that pierce your soul" are often reviled, but, quoting from Lillith's description again, "a well-proportioned figure suggests a graceful body" manages to convey a certain impression without overly imposing on the looker.

One of the reasons that overly imposing descriptions don't work, is that the player will try to conjure up an image of the character when reading the description. The player builds up an understanding of the other characters, of the particular situation, and indeed of the world that s/he finds hirself in. This image before the mind's eye is a very personal construction much akin to the way a reader constructs an image of the characters and the world presented in a novel. When the reader is confronted with a movie made after the book it is often hard to set one's own image aside and enjoy the movie as a movie and not as a movie after the book. Often however, "the book was better" and maybe rightly so, because such is the power of imagination. In the end the goal of a character's description is to intrigue the reader/looker/player and seduce hir into wanting to get to know the character because its description seems natural, plausible and offers an invitation to interaction.

This leads to the second important observation. The character has to be a realistic, believable person. Each player is in part responsible for the re/creation and sustainment of the virtual environment by performing a character that is not only "in theme" with that particular world, but more importantly a character that embodies that world, a character that perpetuates and reinforces the illusion of realism. As Fine reminds us,

> The crucial issue is to create a world that players can accept *as a world,* and which they can become engrossed in. (1983: 81, italics in original)

In a completely fictional world a character made out of text can be anyone or anything you want it to be, but to portray a realistic character you will have to perform your character within the limits of the discourse. The discourse I'm referring to here is not very strictly defined, but it can be illustrated by various practices that are considered either good or bad form, such as the above example of overly imposing descriptions. The players of every virtual world will construct a version of the discourse specific to their world, with its own local past and its own IC and OOC *mores.* The most common elements of these discourses are online and pen-and-paper role-playing games, and various established conventions for synchronous and a-synchronous computer-mediated communication. The discourse that defines Cybersphere is a mix of these sources, to which most notably ideas and conventions of the cyberpunk genre have been added.[30]

The first thing to consider for a character to be convincing is that the character has to be consistent with the theme of the world that one is playing in. In the case of Cybersphere this is a fairly dystopian, highly technologized future:

a cyberpunk world. Faeries, elves and vampires do not exist in such a world, except in imagination. Computer- and nanotechnology not possible by today's standards on the other hand is available in Cybersphere. Implants, neural co-processors and other augmentations such as dermal armor and muscle grafts can be purchased and integrated into one's body. Within the perimeters set by the theme of the virtual world the character must be a realistically possible, believable personality. In Cybersphere you can create a character that has cybernetic implants, but magical powers are off limits. Another important factor for a character to be convincing is that the style of its description must mesh with the established discourse. Unless there is some compelling reason for it, characters on Cybersphere will not be dressed in a medieval fashion and will not speak Shakespearean English. Rather, Cyberspehereans' appearance is defined by a widely shared and refined sense of street punk chique and their linguistic usages reflect the nitty-grittyness of their street-level world. The description of a character after all, should inform the other players, or at least give them some hints, about the kind of person they're about to meet.

This then leads to the third observation Lillith makes. The character must have an expressive/visual personality. The description and the character's personality must somehow work together, so that the other players can "learn" the character by connecting salient details in the description to particular traits and dispositions of that character. The description is thus more than just an objective listing of how someone looks and the way it is read of course depends on the context in which it appears.

How then is Lillith's description more of a characterization than an objective listing of how she looks? Her description, it must be noted, is very descriptive without explicitly stating certain character traits. Lillith explains how it might be read in the context of her personal history and that of Cybersphere in general like this:

```
Lillith (not to be self-praisin') is a good example.. in
ways, I designed her to symbolize feminine strength. [A] lot
of things are expressions of her youth.. clothes etc.. its
the general @desc[31] at the beginning that best lays it out..
The manner of her gaze, and her expressions as described in
the usual 'look' show that the individual is one well-aware
of her strengths and weaknesses, and prepared to use them.
Balance is the sign of someone well-oriented with their
gender. A 'strong' male or female is someone who is attuned
to the strengths of their particular gender, and how to best
use them to exist as a member of that gender.
```

I find it hard to point out a particular gaze or expression in Lillith's description when it is taken out of context and presented more or less by itself, like above in this text. Having interacted with Lillith as a character I know what she is hinting at when she mentions the characteristics that she does.

How this works is maybe best compared to RL. When you meet someone you get a general impression of that person, but there is too much detail to any person to grasp the whole at once. Conversing with that person for a few minutes teaches you more about that person than looking at hir ever will. In retrospect you, often unwittingly, contribute or link particular traits or habits of that person to hir general appearance, making it believable that you knew what s/he was like all along.

The process of getting to know a character starts with the name and description, paying attention to those details that are particularly salient in the description or that you have found to be particularly informative. Graye says, "`I pay particular attention to what is emphasized in another character's description; sometimes, it's stance, sometimes, it's intelligence, other times it's the face, or an overall impression the player wishes to convey with the character.`" Getting to know Lillith and matching the manner of her gaze and her expressions to her description is thus much as Tôsama describes it: a learning process where new information about her character is continually amended to the mental image you have formed when you first met her. The way to meaningfully read a description then, is more than just reading it. Lillith's description can be read as offering sufficient detail to form an image, but at the same time offering enough "openings" where the player can weave hir own experiences with Lillith into the interstices of the description. This makes it possible for the player interacting with Lillith to "characterize" her, instead of being confronted with a cartoon character without emotional or personal depth whose description doesn't offer any openings to act on.

When Eveline first met Lillith she thought she must be an emotionally very disturbed person. What else could the scars crisscrossing Lillith's wrists point to than attempted suicide(s)? Lillith was sitting across the table and I studied her face curiously, swirling the last sip of my latte around in its cup, while listening to the story of how Lillith arrived in New Carthage.

```
Lillith leans closer. "There's no top in my world. It's sterile.
  I'm one of a thousand fetuses in antiseptic baths. Me and all
  the miserable corporate golden children. I want to fall. I want
  to.. hurt."
Eveline leans back and takes another very good look at Lillith,
  slowly forming words out of the cascade of thoughts and
  memories tumbling in her head, "so... you're from the other
  side of the wall...?"
```

Lillith [to Eveline]: Chicago doesn't have a wall like this city. Proper children call us skywalkers. Perhaps I'd see the ground once a month, surrounded by husks of suit and flesh pretending to be men. I recite poetry to mirrors, and I don't dare sing.

Eveline lets her gaze wander over Lillith and stares for a long moment at the scars on her wrist, "skywalkers? a true vertical segregation then... even more vivid than the so called money wall here in Carthage... *nods and points to the scars with her eyes* you were trying to hurt yourself? trying to feel?"[32]

Lillith glances down at her arms, as though noticing the cuts for the first time. She nods. "That's why I'm here. Mother decided she could no longer attempt to live with her terminally depressed, artsy-fartsy, suicidal daughter."

Lillith leans back a bit, smiling in something approximating pride.

Eveline smiles gently at Lillith, "so... finally you got what you wanted from your mother and now you're here, wanting to hurt... no... wanting to live... am i right?"

Lillith widens her eyes beyond the facade of control. "Will you break my fall?"

Eveline's assessment turned out to be correct. Lillith had made several suicide attempts back in NeoChicago, where, as the daughter of a wealthy family, she was being kept like a bird in a golden cage. But having fled from her cage, having taken her fate in her own hands, Lillith now wanted to live, more than anything else. Although she was still learning how, she turned out to be a strongwilled person with a deep inner strength, and maybe not surprisingly so, since she must have put up an incredible fight to finally be able to leave her safe home back in Chicago. The scars thus, so prominently "there" in her description, did not any longer hint at an emotionally unstable person, but rather became indicative of Lillith's newfound inner strength and her will to live life close to who she really was.

It's not easy describing and performing a convincing character, especially not when the "reading" or appreciation of one's character depends on the very idiosyncratic ways in which other players read your description. Being well balanced and attuned to the strengths of one's gender are the most important things that make a convincing character in Lillith's mind.[33] Her criteria are very personal and thoughtful, but they don't quite reflect how players in general read the various character descriptions. While reading a description and constructing a mental image of the character is an inherently personal process, it is possible to discern some general models by which players construct these images. Usually the players assess other characters along the lines of images already present in society, and in the case of Cybersphere through the imagery present in the cyberpunk genre.

Shadowschild's comments on what makes a good female or male description voices some widely shared opinions, most importantly: "`Details details details! Very important.. it is the little stuff that will always give it away.`" Every character has some sort of description and wears some sort of clothing, it is in the details of how they are written that one can find the best clues as to what kind of character one is being confronted with, as Shadowschild explains:

> `I have found, in my experience, that the male players (with both male and female characters) tend to have bad spelling or grammar, spend little time on fine details (such as "aqua" or "sapphire" instead of just "blue") and tend to be a little more concerned with ages.... (saying "about 20ish" instead of just saying "young"). [H]ow many men do you know who know the difference between "aqua", "aquamarine", "teal" and "turquoise", off hand? And of those... how many actually CARE?`

These observations mesh very well with my own, but of course they are not set in stone. There are female players who are bad spellers and there are male players who have meticulously groomed descriptions and speak and act largely grammatically and syntactically correct. Nevertheless, a large part of the male player population of Cybersphere has a description with at least a few linguistic errors that is decidedly utilitarian, lacking the flowery details and careful phrasing that most of the female player population features. It is quite possible that the bad grammar and spelling is correlated to age and education level. The female respondents are on average 3.8 years older than the males, although the difference on Cybersphere is much smaller, the female respondents being only 1 year older on average. When I started my research I focused on gender and didn't include questions about the player's education level in my questionnaire. It would be an interesting line of inquiry to see if there is any correlation between age/education and proper spelling and grammar use in an online role-playing situation, where a lot of the interaction depends not only on correct spelling and grammar, but also on typing and verbalization skills. Of course, the context in which these results have been gathered is a rather specific and fairly small one.

When I further questioned Shadowschild on why these details in the general description and the clothing are so important, the following dialogue ensued:

```
Shadowschild says, "Admittedly... I am American.. and I come from
   an American culture... we do not expect our males to be...
   very.... very umm..... We consider that kind of detail to be
   necessary for female success.. but not for male."
Eveline nods and understands, "That kind of detail is necessary
   to come across as a convincing female character?"
Shadowschild says, "Among other things. It is one thing... by
   itself, I would not commit to saying yea or nay about a
   character... but it is one thing that, combined with others,
   might make me wonder."
```

Shadowschild's comments point to an intriguing question. If the character for some reason is not convincing as a male or female, then what, or rather who is the player behind the character? If, for instance, the description of a female character lacks the flowery language and attention to detail that Shadowschild mentions, does this indicate that this female character is played by a male player? Not necessarily, as Shadowschild says, but it might make you wonder. Of course it's common knowledge that there are quite a lot of cross-gender characters. The sample size admittedly is fairly small, but 60% of the female players and also 60% of the male players reported to (at least once) have played a cross-gender character. Common knowledge also has it that more male players are playing female characters than there are female players who play male characters. This common knowledge is not entirely corroborated by the findings from my questionnaire. Of the Cybersphere players 57% of the female respondents reported to have played a cross-gender character, while 47% of the male respondents reported to have done so (at least once).

Cross-gender characters and the ideas about playing a cross-gender character are an especially interesting subject for my inquiry into the online performance of gender because when discussing cross-gender characters players tend to emphasize, sometimes even polarize, the characteristics they ascribe to the different genders. Players state quite clearly what they think is appropriate or necessary for the performance of a convincing male or female character and what sort of things are dead give-aways. Kessler and McKenna discuss a study done by Birdwhistell, who argues that in everyday interaction people rely on "tertiary sexual characteristics" or such nonverbal behaviors as "facial expression, movement and body posture" (1978: 156). "Primary sexual characteristics" such as genitals are no "critical gender markers" according to Birdwhistell because in everyday life they're usually hidden and "secondary sexual characteristics" such as breasts and facial hair display too much variance from individual to individual to be taken as clearly dichotomous (Kessler and McKenna: 153-154). Kessler and McKenna rightly fault Birdwhistell for *first* sorting people "into one of two gender categories, and only then, after an initial gender attribution was made, were these displays compared" (1978: 156). This way of course the male and female gender categories are established based on the researcher's conscious or unconscious criteria for femininity and masculinity, which inevitably highlights some characteristics, while downplaying others. Another problem Kessler and McKenna see, is that,

> [r]ather than asking people to notice or describe the typical and atypical behaviors of their own and other gender (which, as even Birdwhistell notes, can never result in an exhaustive list), information could be gathered on which, if any, nonverbal behaviors are "conditions of failure." In what nonverbal ways could a person behave such that her/his gender is questioned? [...] If the conditions of failure could be described, then people could be any gender they wanted to be, at any time. (1978: 157)

In my interviews and questionnaire I have posed the basic question about the "conditions of failure" in two complementary ways. Apart from asking the players what it takes for a character to fail at convincing the other player of its "realness," I have also asked the players about what it takes to be a convincing female or male character, even though Kessler and McKenna argue that this only recreates the gender stereotypes. This approach served two functions. On the one hand these questions allowed me to compare and check the answers of the players against one another, while on the other hand both types of questions lead to interesting answers and discussions exactly because we were talking about the construction and performance of femininity and masculinity in/on/through characters in a virtual world and not Real Life.

Why do most players want to know the RL gender of another player? A lot of players say, when asked, that the RL gender of another player doesn't really matter to them as far as role-playing is concerned. Indeed, the whole point of role-playing in a MUD is that you *play a role* and not yourself, something most players seem to acknowledge. In personal communication Penumbra's player said:

```
I don't really go online to socialize. This doesn't mean
that I'm anti-social or contemptuous of people online, but
when I log on, I'm really looking for a shared experience or
some sort of collaborative storytelling. Something
structured, I guess. This is why I like Cybersphere, because
it's like a huge creative zeitgeist where everyone's always
tossing ideas into the mix. It's the textual equivalent of a
mural...
```

Still, most players will ask you about who you are IRL sooner or later, or, if they don't ask you directly, they will more or less consciously evaluate your role-playing in order to make some sense of the player behind the character that they have been interacting with so much. There are two main reasons that players mention that get them interested in the player behind a character. Penumbra comments on the first reason,

> [So] it's not all that important to me what the 'real' gender of another online persona really is. But! I do find myself becoming curious when I really get to 'know' the person online, and find that the person has similar interests, or maybe similar opinions, or when we just start to 'get along'. Then I get an urge to 'relate' to the person behind the screen name, and the fundamental property that allows humans to 'cast' each other and understand other humans is gender. Once you've established gender, the gender allows you to put all your conceptualizations of the other person into context. Without gender, all you have is a jumbled assemblage of impressions and vague ideas about the other person. Now, this isn't necessarily good -- putting a persona into gender context -- because once you've cast a person as 'male' or 'female', then lots of your internal preconceptions immediately start to surface. I think that the whole 'context' issue is pretty much universal (in my limited knowledge of the subject!) because IRL, when you see _anyone_ on the street, one of the very, very first things you notice about them is: 'Male or female?'

The second reason to get curious about who a player is IRL is because the portrayal of a character is a bit "off". Players' interests are piqued and they will look for particular details of the character's performance to assess who the player behind it is. A portrayal that is "off" usually is perceived not to be consistent with the general stereotypes for such a character. For example, a female character that is very assertive, aggressive maybe, or possibly quite the opposite, only focused on sex and just overly sweet and teasing all the time. For a male character it might be that he is too effeminate, interested mostly in romance.

I can't answer nor would I want to second-guess all the players' reasons for inquiring another player's gender, but I feel I can offer a few sentiments that I think play a role in why the RL gender of a player is important. The two most important concerns involved are the suspension of disbelief in a role-playing MUD and the way we construct our identities. Both these concerns hinge on the fact that you don't just *act* your character, but that in order to play your character convincingly you identify with your character up to a certain point. Just like a good movie actor can make us suspend our disbelief, convince us of the reality of hir character by drawing from hir own experiences, so can the player conjure up a believable image of the character. If the actor can't convince us, we just see an actor on the screen acting hir role, and if the player can't convince us, we see a series of messages scrolling up the screen. This "identification" with your character doesn't have to be something deeply emotional (although it can be), but at least you have to be able to relate to what your character experiences and then react as your character would react. The line between RP and RL is not so absolute as the linguistically imposing terms *Virtual* Reality and *Real* Life seem to imply.[34] There is a big, fuzzy, overlapping area of experiences and utterances that encompasses both "virtual" and "real" realities. In this space the player and hir character are intertwined in unexpected ways that allow players to suspend their disbelief or that can make the player realize the fundamental enactedness of it all. As Graye says, "`RP is never wholly objective. If it is, it's not that interesting.`"

If a player can conjure up a character that is convincing s/he will effect a suspension of my disbelief and I will go along as if s/he is real. A lot of elements are very important for this to happen, name, description, role play, and all these have to form a consistent image of the character that you are interacting with. But you interact with more than just the character, however good the player is playing hir. There is always the other player who is as intimately intertwined with hir character just as I am with mine. While the play is play, the interaction is real and the response is not computer-generated but thought up, invented and extended by another player somewhere in the world. And it is this connection, this subtle shift of who is speaking, that makes it important to know who it is behind that character, who it is effecting this suspension of disbelief and drawing me in.

So, even if the portrayal of a character is 'perfect' (if there is such a thing), if you know that this character is played by someone of another gender than that of the character, this influences how you react to the character. George Eliot, a 21 year old female wizard on Cybersphere, who took her name after the nineteenth century author Mary Ann Evans' pen-name, played a male character for a while, named Lusiphur.[35] While she was playing this character she kept up the impression that there was a male player behind Lusiphur. During an interview I asked her why she would want to pretend that she was a guy OOCly.

```
George Eliot says, "I set out to do it... people react very
  differently when they know you're gender-bending."
Eveline asks, "in what way do they react differently?"
George Eliot says, "It's hard to define, but the interaction is
  less authentic... they tend to talk to you as a member of your
  RL gender rather than as your character's gender."
George Eliot says, "They're more reserved... there's still kinda
  a stigma attached to gender-bending to a certain extent,
```

although it applies less to people going my direction than it does to guys playing women."
Eveline asks, "mmm, a stigma. what sort of stigma?"
George Eliot laughs. "Couldn't define it because I don't feel it... what I noticed though is that after people found out I was a chick, a lot of their IC interaction with Luse stopped or changed... women who were hitting on him stopped, for instance. *grin*"

The "stigma" George Eliot is referring to, I think, is the belief that there must be something "wrong" with the player-as-a-person for hir to want to portray a character of another gender, even more so if it becomes clear that the player portrayed hir RL gender other than it 'really is'. Wanting to play a cross-gender character is often taken as the expression of (latent) homosexuality or a sexual perversion where the person playing such a character gets off on experiencing sex through the opposite sex's point of view (or more graphically, point of penetration). The discussion of cross-gender characters almost inevitably turns into a discussion of net.sex, based on the assumption that that is what a player playing a cross-gender character is after. This discussion takes place in a, usually, firmly heterosexual context, in which for instance homosexual acts are seen as unnatural and opposed to the supposedly natural and biologically pre-ordained order of heterosexuality.

There are, of course, those that play cross-gender characters (mostly male-->female) just to get laid, which is sad and pathetic. But there's nothing wrong with it in the course of a normal character.. it's just more role-playing.

This 19 year old male player from Cybersphere illustrates the point that *as a role-playing exercise,* in the course of playing a normal cross-gender character, having net.sex is allowed. However, should the player (and not the character) want to have net.sex as a cross-gender character, then this is "sad and pathetic." Not all players think that having net.sex as a cross-gender character is okay. Quite a few players draw the line at playing a cross-gender character and won't have net.sex as their cross-gender character or with another cross-gender character. The most common sentiment regarding net.sex, regardless of whether there is a cross-gender character involved, is that if it seems appropriate for the state of the relationship of the involved characters and if fits with the characters' normal behavior, then it's okay.

The proclaimed ideal of role-playing is that the player and the character are completely detached, separate identities. "[O]f course, you must detach the character from yourself, otherwise it'll come across with the characteristics of your [the player's] gender," remarked the 19 year old male Cybersphere player in the discussion of net.sex. This ideal however, is constantly and inherently compromised by the fact that the player is very much emotionally involved with hir character. While in fact a large percentage of the players at one time or another have played a cross-gender character, the fact that the virtual world is embedded in the larger whole of a heterosexually biased society causes a stigma to be applied to those players who try to seriously play a cross-gender character. IC and OOC thus aren't so easily separable, even though the helpfiles urge you not to mix them up too badly with this statement: "`After all, you wouldn't want someone walking into a wet dream and asking for directions to your pineal gland, would you?`" The difference between IC and OOC isn't wholly objective and that's what makes role-playing interesting; it allows the player to experience what it would be like to be hir character, to be emotionally affected like hir character would be and to play out hir emotional states through hir character.

If the player's identity shapes the character and the experiences of the character affect the player, it stands to reason that we should also consider the effects of the fundamental uncertainty of never being totally sure of another player's gender on the ways we relate to ourselves and others. If I suspend my disbelief, if I let myself be seduced by another player to do so, I have to put a lot of trust in that player. The fact is that, even while I know that the character and the player should not be confused with one another, I know that s/he must also be that strange mix of player and character, of self and other. I relate to hir on basis of a trust that s/he and hir character are somehow compatible, somehow one-and-the-same-even-though-divided-in-presentation. It is hard to trust a player when you don't trust hir character and if you do trust the character it's all the more difficult if that trust is betrayed by the player. It is thus important to know the player, or at least the gender of the player, behind those characters that you interact with most intimately.

Shadowschild pointed out the importance of details of the description. If initially there is no certain way to tell what another player's gender is, then trying to determine that unknown player's gender by the way s/he described hir character presupposes that there is a difference between how a man and a woman would describe a particular type of character. More specifically, one would have to presume that there are particular ways in which a woman would describe female or male characters and how a man would describe male or female characters. In essence this presupposes that men and women "speak" differently and hence will automatically use their different ways of speaking when describing their character, whether it is a female or a male character. Believing that one could determine whether a description is written by a man or a woman also presupposes that however close one can get to speaking exactly as the other gender, there will always remain a difference that will be recognizable. Thus, when a player reads a description for clues about the gender of the player behind it, s/he will use hir everyday, common sense knowledge of how men and women speak.

Interestingly enough most players pick up on the same sort of characteristics that are believed to be indicative of a cross-gender character. The characteristics that players put forward form a stereotype of sorts in themselves. Especially the buxom, scantily clad female character intent on sex, that is believed to be played by a hormone-driven teenage boy, is an image that is frequently put forward.

```
Vampina
A young woman with an unconcealably large pair of breasts. They
  jut out from her body for feet, covering the entire front of
  her torso. Her hips flare out nicely, and she walks surely.She
  has an almost girlish face, soft and oval, with large green
  eyes looking out from a frame of long, blond hair. Hair
  cascades down over her smooth shoulders. A huge pair of breasts
  leap from her chest. Lage and round, with large, erect nipples,
  they bounce and jiggle as she moves. Something around a size 93
  tripple-H, the cover her entire upper torso. Most of her
  midsection is obscured by her huge breasts, buy you can make
  out a well- muscled tight stomach. Her hips are perfectly
  shaped and proportioned. Her pelvic bones form aperfect,
  visible V shape, her hips flaring out just below her waise. Her
  buttox is tight and firm, and leads into her strong back
  muscles. Long, smooth legs support her. Her large, stiff thigh
  muscles taper down to small ankles, and all the skin is well
  tanned, even what you can see of her inner thighs.
She is in excellent health.
Vampina is empty-handed.
```

Vampina's description mirrors the stereotypical teenage-boy-describing-sex-goddess-image quite exactly and even features the 'obligatory' spelling and grammar errors. In fact, the whole image is so over the top that I think it's done tongue-in-cheek. I'm not entirely sure though. Vampina was around for not more than a month and I haven't interacted with her in that time. Actually, I have mostly just seen her "sleeping" on the streets, the character abandoned because the player simply logged out and 'forgot' to take hir character to a suitable sleeping place.

For male characters played by a female player the stereotype is somewhat less well defined and seems to fall into two kinds of characters, the muscle-bound Schwarzenegger type and the friendly guy. I must emphasize that virtually all players refer to these images of cross-gender characters when they are asked how one could recognize them. Often players also note that these kinds of characters are easy to spot and not the most thought-out and well performed characters. With more complex and better performed characters it's harder to see whether a man or a woman is playing the character, but, as Shadowschild noted, it is generally pointed out that in the finer details recognizable differences in "female" and "male" style can be detected. Graye names a few areas of interest he pays particular attention to:

> In a character's gender, I look for emphasis on sexual parts of the body, syntax and word use when describing the character (ass vs rear, tits vs chest, muscular vs built, chiseled features vs no features at all), and frequently the clothing a character wears, and how IT is described.

Aragorn's description below seems to be a good example of a well described male character. The chiseled features are quite prominent and although the description doesn't mention bulging muscles, one cannot fail to notice that it would probably be unwise to try to push this person around.

```
Aragorn
He notices your glance, somewhat subtly. His emerald green eyes
  travel to the floor before ascending upwards to level with
  your gaze confidently. He offers no challenge, no judgment
  with his stare. Mere acknowledgment followed by a soul probing
  smile as he tests your personality for response. He shakes his
  head, his brow furrowing slightly as he pushes a stray strand
  of matted blonde hair behind his right ear. Glancing away,
  this tall, gracefully wiry man seems to almost inaudibly
  "hmmph" to himself. His enitre demeanour changes with the
  blink of an eye.
Rigid and taught, yet still relaxed, his stance moulds to the
  paradoxical state of readiness. He scans the room, as though
  searching for something. As quickly as his assertiveness
  arose it disappears once again. Whether he found what he was
  searching for, or he remembered something different remains
  to be said though. He looks to you again, quizzically,
  though still not agressively. He shrugs quite contentedly
  and returns to his own world with a smile and a lilt of the
  head.
A gently chiseled jaw line hides casually under what appears to
  be a few days stuble. A dark black, grey trench coat hangs
```

> easily from Aragorn's frame. His's shoulders seem to roll unconciously under the material, comfortable in the solace its full cover brings from the elements. The hem, frayed and tattered hangs at calf level, stray bits of synth-cotton coming away here and there. A pair of faded denim jeans adds to the lay-about-synth-surfer image that appears to remain the quintessence of Aragorn's nature. Its hems too are frayed and tattered, white cotton peeling away and falling down unkemptly. Dirty, black soled feet support him steadily.
>
> He is in excellent health.
>
> Aragorn is holding a beer.

In tune with the cyberpunk theme of Cybersphere, Aragorn is painted as a rough and ready man, without overly emphasizing "broad shoulders," "bulging muscles," or "piercing eyes." His clothing is described relatively straight forward, the most obvious detail being the frayed hems of his coat and pants, which "[add] to the lay-about-synth-surfer image." All in all the whole description exudes an air of a confident, probably fairly solitary and possibly dangerous individual. Aragorn is played by a male player and while it is detailed and well written, it doesn't overly focus on fabrics, colors, etc. "Green" or "emerald" eyes are a much more common feature in the character descriptions than IRL. This is probably because green eyes are considered special IRL and thus they function as 'natural' attention getters.

The detail brought forward in Aragorn's description is all geared towards making him a "tough guy" and his clothing underscores those qualities of his personality quite adequately. The clothing of a character plays an important role in defining a character. Clothing can be read as a socially meaningful system and especially in the cyberpunk genre one can find important clues about the character's "archetype" in its description. Graye further comments on the use of clothing in the characters' descriptions:

> Clothing is often indicative of a player's attitude toward their character and whether or not the gender of the character is the same as the player's IRL gender. Example: Many men who play female characters, from my experience, will describe the female characters to fit a personal fantasy. Frequently, they'll do it tastefully enough that it'll be difficult to tell if it's really a man behind the woman, as it were. But often, the clothes the character will wear will largely clash with the attitude and the IC persona of a character; I've rarely known female intellectuals that are particularly strong-willed and into comfort to go out

for extremely revealing leathers or latex, but this happens, on occasion.

A good example of Graye's remarks on how men often describe a female character to fit their personal fantasies is Maia.

Maia

Her face is a beautiful round shape with slightly high cheek bones and honey colored skin. You notice her striking green eyes fixed on you, almond shaped and offset by her dark hair, cascading down to her shoulders. The cut of her hair is such that it is tapered, exposing her lovely neck. She flashes you a charming smile and raises one eyebrow curiously. Maia appears to be of Japanese heritage.

Around Maia's neck is a black leather cat collar, a round brass bell gleams in the light. It gingles lightly as she moves. As you look at Maia you would swear that she is a large tiger. The beautiful markings of a bengal tiger cover her body perfectly, the outline of her breasts and beautiful curves draw your eye all the way to her feet. The soft fur glistens in the light of The Haven. Maia's tail swishes back and forth curiously as she looks at you then lets out a soft purr; her bright green eyes grining misheviously at you. On her delicate hands are a finely crafted pair of leather gloves, are cuffed to the wrist. Adorning her feet are finely crafted short black leather boots that are cuffed.

She is in excellent health.

Maia (VF) is empty-handed.

While Maia's general description features a "lovely neck" I think that it is not so much out of the ordinary that it couldn't have been written by a woman. Notice, by the way, her green eyes. Maia's clothing however is not something that a woman would typically have her character wear. Maia's "big kitty" look sexualizes her in a fashion that is most commonly associated with a man's way of describing. Sexualizing the character however is not necessarily an indication that a female character is played by a male player. Maera, for example, was played by George Eliot's player, who is female.

Maera

A slender woman about six feet tall, with pale skin and black hair that hangs in rippling waves down to her waist. She moves with the self-assurance of someone used to taking care of herself.

```
Long, jet black hair frames Maera's pale face and offsets her
   indigo blue eyes before rippling down her back.  A thin tattoo
   made up of intricately intertwined strands of rainbow colors
   encircles her throat like a choker. Maera's black leather
   jacket creaks and jingles softly as she moves, and you glimpse
   the legend "Fuck the Police" painted across the back. A deep
   black velvet dress clings to the lush curves of Maera's body as
   though it was painted onto her skin.  The neckline drops low,
   revealing the pale, delicate skin of her full cleavage, and the
   bottom hem falls just low enough to be decent, but not so low
   to avoid revealing that her long legs do, indeed, go all the
   way up.  Her hands are slim and strong, with long fingers and
   glossy black nails.  Her legs are mostly bare to the world, the
   lattice of a pair of fishnet stockings deep black against her
   pale skin.  Maera's height is boosted by a pair of black patent
   leather ankle boots that sport a pair of ridiculously thin
   three inch stiletto heels.
She is in excellent health.
Maera is empty-handed.
```

Maera's skimpy dress, deep cleavage, stiletto's and fishnet stockings are offset by a few characteristics that make her more than just a two-dimensional, highly sexualized image of a woman. She's fairly tall, moves with confidence and the tattoo in combination with the leather jacket with "Fuck the Police" painted on the back lend her a certain determination and posture. Maera's player later contrasted her "public" description with her "private" description, showing how the apparently clashing aspects of Maera's public description can be understood as visualizations of an inner, deeper, more private self of the character.

```
Maera, in retrospect, did display one characteristic that I
generally use to tag cross gendered characters: her clothing
(and thus the 'public' description most people saw) was
always fetishistic and extremely sexualized, i.e. thigh-high
black patent leather stiletto heeled boots, black leather
catsuits, extremely skimpy and revealing dresses, etc etc.
As a matter of fact, the first pair of those boots was
created specifically for Maera at my request. :) Her nudity
messages (the 'private' description, seen only among her IC
lovers), on the other hand, were much less stereotypical of
a cross gendered character.
```

While she is dressed to kill, Maera's sexualized presence is thus quite a bit different from Maia's.

The next statement from Graye's typically long and detailed exposé details what can go 'wrong' if a woman plays a male character.

> `In other cases, a woman playing a man will emphasize the wrong parts of a man's description; patterns on clothing, and materials, whereas most men who play men ICly, in my experience, rarely bother with that sort of thing. How a character appears, how a character is garbed, and the language used in the portrayal of the character is important, as well.`

It is interesting to note that the characteristics deemed indicative of a woman describing a female character are transferred to how she will describe a male character. Attention to detail, patterns, materials and colors of clothing seem to surface as particularly indicative of a female player. However, not all female players automatically describe their male characters with lots of attention to detail.

Lusiphur, who was played by George Eliot's player, seems to fit the general mould for a male-described-male-played-character quite well. Lusiphur's description doesn't stand out particularly by the 'standards' mentioned for recognizing a female player's description, so it might be said that this character is a successful impersonation. This is confirmed by the fact that George Eliot's player played Lusiphur for quite a while without people knowing it was her playing, even keeping up the impression that she was male IRL. The description above on the left is the one she had written for him when she had just created this character. It's interesting to see this original description (on the left) next to the one (on the right) that Lusiphur sported when he had 'matured' a bit. Small changes can make a big difference in the overall appearance of a character.

The images all these descriptions call forth are in the first place inspired by the cyberpunk genre. If one takes the sourcebook for the Cyberpunk 2020 role-playing game as a lead, one easily recognizes the archetypes it describes. Rockerboys: rebel rockers who use music and revolt to fight authority; solos: hired assassins, bodyguards, killers and soldiers; netrunners: cybernetic computer hackers; techies: renegade mechanics and doctors; medias: newsmen and reporters who go to the wall for the truth; cops: maximum lawmen on mean 21st century streets; corporates: slick business raiders and multi-millionaires; fixers: deal makers, smugglers, organizers and information brokers; nomads, road warriors and gypsies who roam the highways (Pondsmith et al. 1990: 4-24).

On the other hand, the way a character's gender is incorporated in these descriptions is primarily derived from more or less stereotypical images already present in Western society. While the characteristics for recognizing a cross-

Lusiphur

A young man, about 5'8", with a slender, muscular build, who moves with wary caution, always keeping his back to a wall.
Lusiphur's ice blue eyes watch the world from behind locks of jet black hair that have escaped from its untidy ponytail. The muscles of Lusiphur's chest and abdomen are outlined by his soft, tight black t-shirt. Corded muscles run the length of his arms, and his forearms are a mass of knife-fighting scars. Lusiphur's hands have a nimble, capable look to them, and sport multiple scars from a variety of weapons, including, you think, lit cigarettes. Lusiphur's sooty grey jeans appear to be perilously close to simply giving up the ghost and falling apart. Lusiphur's feet are protected by a pair of non-descript black cowboy boots, comfortably sprung in all the right places.
He is in excellent health.
Lusiphur is holding a beer and a credstick.

Lusiphur

A young man, about 5'8" tall, with a compact, muscular build. He moves with fluid, confined motions, and never puts his back to a door.
Lusiphur's ice blue eyes watch the world warily from behind an untidy collection of shoulder length black hair. Hanging from a strap across his shoulders is a large black sword scabbard. Lusiphur's heavy black leather trenchcoat creaks as he moves. The upper part of the back has been painted with a copy of the playing card 'Jack of Hearts'. Lusiphur is wearing a pair of dull black, leather bracers that have many nasty looking chrome spikes going down the back them. Lusiphur's hands have a nimble, capable look to them, and sport multiple scars from a variety of weapons, including, you think, lit cigarettes. Lusiphur's jeans are mostly black, only faded a little at the knees and seams. Lusiphur's feet are protected by a pair of non-descript black cowboy boots, comfortably sprung in all the right places.
He is in excellent health.
Lusiphur is empty-handed.

gender character largely point to the extremes of gender images, they do indicate the more subtle ways in which gender is evaluated. However, the more intelligently and subtly a character is performed, the harder it becomes to adequately assess the other player's gender by merely scrutinizing hir character's description. It is even possible, as George Eliot's player did with Lusiphur, to convince others that IRL one is of another gender than one truly is. This however does not detract from the fact that players continue to use various strategies as outlined above to judge the convincingness of characters. Cross-gender characters are somehow considered less real than 'normal' characters. This has to do with the fact that a player does not merely role play hir character, but that s/he has to put a part of hirself into the performance to make it realistic. Even if one is a good role-player, it's not easy to set one's preconceptions aside and the fact that one knows that the male character one is interacting with is played by a female player actually influences how one interacts with that character, even if that's not according to the ideal of role-playing which says that things like that shouldn't play a role.

However, not only cross-gender characters are subjected to the ways a character is judged on its convincingness. All characters, in order to be 'good' characters, are so scrutinized and even 'normal' characters must adhere to the conventions that describe how a convincing male or female character ought to act. George Eliot's player, in fact, commented on the fact that she was rumored to be male IRL because of her character and presentation, both ICly and OOCly, on Cybersphere.

> I was often accused of being male, both as George Eliot and as my female character, Maera, -especially- when I would get combative with other players. The accusers were pretty equally distributed among male and female players who I antagonized quite cheerfully, feeling that they were idiots anyway. The rumour may still be circulating for all I know, I debunked it several times when chatting OOCly with other players. [...] I believe it was the combination of her [Maera's] provocative clothing, her aggressive personality, and the equally aggressive persona I presented as George Eliot, who was widely known as my wiz, that lead people to the conclusion that I was, in fact, a guy. *grin* I can provide numerous references that I'm not, and my rather aggressive IRL personality and conversational styles at least don't cause the same confusion... ;>

In RL George Eliot's player isn't taken for a man despite her aggressive personality and conversational style, but online, lacking other points of reference, her "unwomanly" behavior is seen as an indication to think of her as a man IRL. It is thus possible for a player to even fail at presenting a character that is of the same gender as the player hirself. Kessler and McKenna say that,

> [g]iven basic trust regarding gender, successfully passing transsexuals, by virtue of being successful, will be impossible to locate... To be successful in one's gender is to prevent any doubt that one's gender is objectively, externally real. (1978: 158)

While there are plenty examples of people successfully passing as the other gender IRL, this is only partially possible online. Online there is no basic trust regarding gender, quite the contrary, there is a basic distrust of gender online. While one can be highly successful in preventing any doubt regarding one's gender by adhering strictly to the various rules and guidelines for what is deemed appropriate, online there is no way in which one can ultimately claim to be in possession of the appropriate objectively and externally real body. Online too, the body is considered the ultimate defining principle of gender and in the absence of a real body, the virtual, substituted body will be scrutinized for clues regarding the gender of the "real" body behind the keyboard. This virtual body is regarded in the same way as a body IRL, the same rules apply. The main difference is the fact that IRL there is a basic trust in the fact that if a body appears to be of a certain gender it *is* that gender, while online there is no such fundamental trust.

Meet the Rabbit

I might have known trouble was coming. It was inevitable, a matter of time really. Maybe I was just naive or maybe I was too confident, but somehow I had always thought that I would recognize trouble and would be able to do the right thing. To act morally... I was so innocent it ties my tummy in a knot to think of it now. Once you have crossed that line, that naive moral straw that you were holding on to, only cynicism remains. Maybe it is just this forsaking of your own, deeply felt moral boundaries that makes it possible to truly understand what cynicism is.

Anyway... I was in this dive bar, the Syndrome. At that time it more or less was my living room since the apartment had become too crowded for the three of us to share. Merlin was up to his eyeballs into some heavy shit and just used our place to crash, sleeping with his arm on an Uzi. I wasn't particularly keen on getting killed in my sleep, caught in a gang fight I had nothing do with. I would fight back-to-back with Merlin any day, but bleeding to death in my own bed, no thanks. And Arri... my sweet Arrienne, she seemed to have lost it. I couldn't take her erratic behavior and violent outbursts any longer. One moment we would be having the most incredible sex and the next moment she'd be running around the room, getting all geared up, totin' a machinegun.

"Let's hunt," she'd say. "Such and so just has to go down today. He rubbed some people the wrong way and besides... he's a prick."

The one time she managed to persuade me to come with her, she dragged me across town, her eyes frantically scanning the crowds. She ducked in and out of the shittiest bars all the way up and down Joseki. With every minute she was getting more revved and I'm still glad we never found who we were looking for then. I wasn't afraid of her, but I was very much afraid for her. The whole situation was something I didn't want to think about, something I tried to shut out.

So there I was, having a coffee in the Syndrome, talking to Tôsama, who, in this whirl of people apparently gone completely mad, had stayed reassuringly sane. Since the moment we met, we had developed a mutual rapport. We teased each other, teased ourselves with the thought that something more than cheeky dialogue and meaningful glances might exist between us. At the same time though, we both knew that going any further than this game was impossible and maybe this was exactly why we were even playing it. Tôsama had just introduced me to a girl he had met the other day. Freya was just the kind of girl that was his type... very feminine and sweet, but with a certain determination to her. Tôsama was still making introductory remarks when I received a message and with a quick flutter of my eyelids I accessed my communications implant.

I think I kept a straight face or maybe Tôsama's attention was all directed towards Freya, but he didn't notice my amazement. I stared out the window, my heart skipping a beat, wondering what a man like mr. simon would want to contact me for. The biggest crime lord in town just commed me saying hello. Surely that was a mistake, a technical glitch... it couldn't be otherwise. A second message arrived and mr. simon *was* definitely talking to me. It took me a second or so before I could focus on what he had asked, but I remember his exact words to this day. "I have something the VF might want and kinda like... would you like to hear my offer..."

What could mr. simon have to offer the Violent Femmes? We weren't exactly a gang, more like a safe haven for the women of this town, and besides, we hadn't had any real trouble with anyone lately. And why would he be talking to me? Alaria was our leader and I had only joined the ranks of the VF a few weeks ago. It was not like I had much of a say in things yet. I had to com him back though, I couldn't just stand here thinking forever and so I commed him a simple yes. I'd better play this cool and see what he had to say. Maybe what he had to offer was indeed interesting for the VF and that would surely get me some credit with the other members. Within three seconds of my com-message my cellphone rang. I pulled it out and smiled apologetically to Tôsama and Freya and ducked into one of the booths at the far end of the room.

I flipped open my phone after the third ring and when I put it to my ear I heard a dark and resolute voice simply say, "Hello..."

I took a deep, mental breath and said, "Hi... this is Evie. You have a nice voice I must say."

I'm not sure I heard simon grin, but I think he might have been when he answered. "Thank you... I will be right to the point... a NCPD squad car, drivers cleared and a set of keys. You want?"

My mind did a double take. A NCPD squad car? How'd he get his hands on that? The NCPD had completely collapsed after the precinct had been bombed, but driving a squad car about town would surely mean quite a bit of trouble with some ex-NCPD people who felt more entitled to it than the VF. It was a really great catch though, but it wasn't up to me to decide if the VF would want the car.

Disappointed I answered, "Ow... Well, I'm not that high up in the hierarchy. Actually, I think only Alaria can make these decisions."

simon immediately shot back at me, "I'm not asking about the VF. I heard that *you* are it. I am willing to deal with you if you would like..." He paused and then continued, "I'm not at this moment willing to deal with Alaria. She is too rash and acts a little out of the normal order of biz I like to conduct."

I stared at the cheap formica table I was sitting at and tried to think, not to much avail. I felt the silence drag on and lamely answered, "Eh... I'm still coming off the booze, had a rough night. Sorry, but I don't think I have the cash for it laying around."

My mind dragged itself around in the same self-centered circles and I thought I'd better say something more to simon.

"I like it very much that you think of me, let's have dinner next time, okay? We can chat about more pleasant things," I babbled.

The phone remained silent for a moment, except for a little static.

"Hmm... how would you like it as a gift?"

His voice seemed softer now, sweeter, but at the same time he still sounded very much businesslike. His tone of voice caught me off guard and warily I shot back at him, "Oh, really? And there are no strings attached? Like, for instance, some mad ex-NCPD people?"

Immediately I regretted the way I snapped at him and in my sweetest voice I said, "Withdraw your honor... yes."

The phone remained silent and I stared at the greasy, chipped formica, thinking I had just blown it completely. I could have sold that car for a nice price to one gang or another. I could have made enough on that thing to pay for razor-claws at a respectable clinic and I just completely blew it. Then I heard muffled voices in the background and a few times a door slammed shut. The conversation grew more heated but I couldn't make out what was being said. Finally the argument ended and another door slammed shut, the sound of it echoing in something like a vast, empty warehouse. I listened closely, but after that I didn't hear anything more.

A drop of sweat ran down my neck. After waiting another minute I coughed and said into the phone, "Uh... hello? Is this line still open? Can you hear me?"

I heard the soft sound of the phone being picked up from a table and simon's voice, "Yes. Give me a few..."

The synthleather was cool against my skin as I leaned back in the booth, phone to my ear. It was like listening to a shell at the beach. I don't think there was anything I could hear, but I imagined that the silence had an echo, a slow, hollow echo. The image of a huge, empty warehouse was so vivid that I almost jumped up from my seat when simon got back on the phone again.

"Okay... where can I drop it off," he grinned.

I think I mostly stifled a nervous giggle when I answered, "How about in front of the Syndrome? Is there, by the way, anything in particular that I should know about driving a squad car?"

"I think not. I shall drive with you a while and show you how it works..."

Smiling to myself I answered him, "Thanks."

"I shall be there in a few. Is that to your liking?" Simon asked.

"Yes, most definitely. I'll be outside the Syn."

simon didn't disconnect so I kept the phone to my ear and got up. Tôsama and Freya were engaged in an animated discussion so I waved goodbye to them from across the room. The heat and humidity draped themselves on my shoulders and sucked away my breath as I stepped outside. I scanned the street and the crowded sidewalk and decided to lean against the drainpipe that separated the Syndrome from Arabica's coffeeshop next door. Maybe not the best place to be waiting for someone... too many people had died on the sidewalk in front of the Syn. Some shot over the silliest of arguments, others caught in a hail of lead from a drive-by shooting, and then there was the time the Syndrome got bombed.

There was no way telling what exactly simon had in mind, offering me the squad car like this. I had heard gruesome stories about how he had literally ripped apart some of his girlfriends whom he suspected to have betrayed him. On the other hand there were those stories telling of his legendary cold-bloodedness that had saved him from seemingly hopeless situations.

The cellphone was hot in my sweaty hand. "I am curious... so someone told you that 'I am it'. That begs the question of who said that to you and what 'it' means. Maybe you can answer that for me, or is it confidential?" I grinned into the phone, not really expecting an answer.

The connection was terminated with a soft beep and the squad car came around the corner, its tires squealing and the back drifting. The big black man behind the wheel slammed the brakes and the car skidded to a stop at the curb, the engine whining in a high pitch. He tooted the horn and when I stepped forward the doors unlocked with a solid metal clunk. I looked around, but nobody paid any particular attention to me or the fairly impressive arrival of the squad car, so I just got in. The moment I pulled the door shut the doors locked and he pulled away from the curb, burning rubber.

I grabbed the armrest as he dragged the car through a corner and looked at him more closely now. From his voice on the phone I had thought he was a white guy, but here I was sitting next to a big black man who spoke without any trace of an accent. Piercing black eyes shot a glance at me. His whole head was covered in red fishbone tattoos, his nose covered with an assortment of piercings, giving him a particularly fierce look. He was wearing a black, leather bodysuit and over that a pair of pants that shone with black and grey fibers. He had a small black backpack in his lap and half slung across his shoulder, half parked next to the drivers' seat was a long, slightly curved, black sheath, ornately carved with strange, gold inlaid oriental symbols. I wondered why people called him "The White Rabbit."

"Someone told you that you were it?" he asked, keeping his eyes on the road.

I blinked at simon, "I can vaguely remember you saying something of that ilk on the phone. Not wanting to deal with the VF, with Alaria, but that I was it."

He took his eyes off the road for a moment and looked me over, "Ahhh... The VF and I have not seen eye to eye ever, WLI and the VF made a pact not to cross the other. Alaria has crossed that line... many of your sisters have willingly followed her across that line, except for you. You knew nothing of the deal or the breaking of that deal, hence you are it."

simon noticed my blank expression and added, "WLI... Waydown Labs Inc."

I smiled at simon, hoping that my droopy eyelids did not betray the dullness the cheap alcohol had left in the back of my head, "Ah... yes, I have managed to stay comfortably ignorant of politics the short period I've been here."

mr. simon hummed noncommittingly, "I have just gotten back into town myself."

The streets here were almost completely deserted. He pulled up at the curb and slipped the gear into neutral. He looked me over again and it was only then that I realized I was still wearing the clothes I had dressed in for clubbing. I figured he must have taken me for some sort of bimbo, all dressed up in tight latex pants and this hot lace up vest.

"Slide on over behind the wheel and I'll sit there."

I grinned rather self-consciously and we switched places. simon grinned along with me and urged me to just drive about town a bit. The car had a smooth, powerful ride just like you'd expect from a specially tuned squad car. simon stared out the window at the dilapidated buildings and I softly sang my driving song, "Twenty-five tons of hardened steel... rolling down on ordinary wheels..."

When we drove down Fuji simon turned to me, "Are you willing to be my contact for the VF?"

I stared at the brake-lights in front of me and drummed on the steering wheel with my fingers, "Well, I don't really carry that much clout, but Alaria and I seem to get along just fine. I can try... do my best for you. As I understand the VF, or Alaria messed things up a bit?"

Midtown was much busier than Fuji.

"Correct. Alaria has had the sentence of death put on her head. I have never chosen to act that punishment out."

I sucked in some air, making a soft whistling sound, "Ohh..."

simon studied my face. The engine droned on.

Eventually simon spoke again, "The VF right now is a sliver of what they once were. Do you think your sisters could find a use for a few LAW rockets and a few railguns?"

I kept a straight face. LAW rockets and railguns? Jesus H. Christ. You could practically destroy a whole city block with those things, let alone what damage you could do to a convoy or another gang's headquarters. This could really get me some credit with the other VF members, considering the options we'd been discussing for the VF lately. simon of course was right when he said that the influence of the VF in this city was seriously declining. I drove the car along Bayfront, which seemed to stretch out infinitely and decided to play straight with simon.

"Well," I said, "can I trust you to keep this to yourself? Seeing that we are forming some kind of alliance here..."

simon nodded soberly, "I never cross on biz..."

I lowered my voice, "Okay... among the VF there is a discussion about reforming the VF into an intelligence slash mercenary group. This is something we can be good at because we can have access to the men in this town, if we want to. What still has to be worked out are the allegiances some of the members have with other groups in town."

simon folded his hands in his lap, his face expressionless, "Lemme guess... you wanna make a trade?"

I nodded, "But as of yet I can't offer anything concrete. I'm just telling you where things are heading for the VF, but if this goes through there'd be some serious business in it."

"Are you on the up and up?" he asked, almost sounding dangerous now.

I stared at the road slipping away under the car, "Yes. That's why I say I can't promise anything... because I just can't."

"I find you to be a very lovely looking flower and I would hate to have something happen to you. Men as you say will sex whatever they feel will give it up. I'm not a mere man and I find the little games long winded." simon coughed, "One time offer. I will give you 100K right now, to be my spy on the VF... and in the VF."

I shot a glance at simon, biting my lip. His offer meant more money than I had ever seen. It also meant giving up the people who had taken me in as one of their own and my affiliation with the VF had without a doubt saved my life in at least two situations already. I had to buy some time, get some time to think this over...

I nodded seriously, "Yes, well... that's an interesting offer..."

"200K and weekly payments of 50K."

I looked at simon and he looked back at me with a blank face and he said, "But then I own you. I will protect you even if all falls apart. A personal aid to myself, for life... or until we part ways."

I have never been good at making quick decisions and I really wanted to think this through. Was I willing to give up my relatively safe life as a member of the VF and make more money than I could possibly spend? Was I really even considering of turning on the VF?

I needed time to think, but the only thing I could come up with was a lame, "So, who else is involved with WLI then?"

"Do you really wish to know? The closer you get the harder it gets to walk away." He sounded confident now, as if he was home free. I didn't like the sound of it, but I couldn't think of any way out right now. I pulled the car up at the curb. I just couldn't think and drive at the same time. Not like this. I turned and looked at simon, finding his eyes among the fishbone tattoos and I tried to see what his eyes were saying to me.

"Is this to test my loyalty to the VF? Or is this for real?"

simon squinted, "I don't mess around on biz. It just makes it longer and harder to get what I want."

Slowly my brain started to make some sense out of this whole situation, "So if you don't get what you want from me, you'll get it elsewhere, right?"

"Now I think you're starting to see how I work," he said. Had he been a cat he would have purred from pleasure. I think he knew he had me. I think he knew all along that he would have me. I think I knew it too, but I was not willing to acknowledge it yet.

"Last question," I tried again, "what about the owning part? What does that comprise...?"

simon smiled happily and I grinned uncertainly.

"It is a known fact," he said slowly, enjoying the fact that people knew things like this, "that I 'keep' lovely things around me... people... You would have the life most can only dream of. You can come and go and if anyone crosses you... you are one of mine... they die."

I sat there. I just sat there and he reached out with his hand and ran his finger over my cheek.

He wetted his lips, "Sex is not something I think should be paid for... I'm sorry."

I think he chuckled when he said that. I just know that I felt enormously relieved. Slowly words returned to me and my cheek felt numb as if his finger had silenced the nerves where he had touched my skin.

"Maybe for the better," I grinned, "I tend to fall for women instead of men."

"That's cool. I once was almost removed by a lady of the night. I hardly ever let my soul's wishes turn into food for the flesh. I have seen too many fall under the sheets after their last hard fuck."

simon leaned forward, took my cold hands in his and lowering his head he placed a soft kiss on my fingers. Then he took out his credstick, put his thumb on the plate, the lo-glo lettering shimmering between his fingers and I heard my own credstick beep when it accepted simon's payment. He unlocked the door and swung it open.

Suddenly this all didn't seem like such a good idea anymore and I realized that while I thought I was happily playing along with simon, he had been playing me all along.

"Wait," I scrambled for words. "This will take my freedom away! I can give you info for free if you will let me be free."

simon stepped out of the car. "I think you will find life is going to get much better for you. Have a nice night and enjoy the car," he said before closing the door.

Despite his imposing figure he immediately disappeared into the crowd on the sidewalk, leaving me at the wheel of the car. I just couldn't believe it. He had played me like a six year-old. I took out my credstick. 200K... I locked the doors of the car. 200K! What about the VF? I couldn't let anyone know where this money came from... Jesus...

I commed him, "I didn't say yes, did I? Let's just see how things go. If you're smart, you'll keep quiet about this... and so will I."

He commed back. "If I am smart??? If you're smart you would know that there is a log of that transaction, anyone who has a reason to go looking will find that you were paid 200K by me. I suggest you worry less about me and more about yourself. I have nothing to loose and everything to gain. As do you."

I swallowed and replied, "Ah... how silly of me. How could I forget..." I put the car in gear, pulled away from the curb and drove into town.

Role-Playing

> Maybe next time use your eyes and look at me
> I'm a drama queen if that's your thing baby
> I can even do reality
>
> —Geri Halliwell, *Look at me*

Eventually, role-playing is what it is all about. It is both the substance and the goal of the game. After coming up with a character-concept, a name and a suitable description the objective is to go out amongst the other characters and role-play. The character is not just a static image, the character has to be animated. It has to live and it has to be lived for that is the character's purpose. Role-playing is hard to describe; in my experience the only way to truly grasp what it is about, is to experience it hands-on, to play a character yourself. Because that may not be an option right here and now, I hope that the preceding pieces of prose and the more theoretical explanations have nevertheless painted a picture of the extensiveness and engrossment of the role-playing experience.

The world of the game is created in particular instances, like for example the way simon mentions WLI. Waydown was a character that had long since gone when Evie and simon were driving around in the squad car. He had been running an operation called Waydown Labs Inc., but it had ceased to function after his 'departure' for all intents and purposes. Eveline had gathered this minimal information, but other than that she didn't know the first thing about WLI and its history. This knowledge and the realization that there must be a whole history behind it, is what simon invokes by referring to WLI when he brings up the agreement between WLI and the VF. simon in effect appropriates the right to call the VF on this agreement, and by doing so simon implies, creates, recreates and invokes in Eveline a sense of history, interconnectedness and scope of the world that goes way beyond the very limited here and now of simon and Eveline together in a squad car. The world would be an empty shell without the characters remembering its history and giving meaning to all the little nooks and crannies it offers. I often went down to the cemetery to think.

Decrepit Graveyard

The razorwire fence was put up only after the old cemetery had been vandalized from a skinhead rally last decade. Now the place is deserted. Weeds have long ago overtaken fallen tombstones, and the neomarble crypts, their doors torn off, look like gasping death itself. Off in one corner, though, there is a tombstone that looks to be newer, the letters still sharp on its surface. The stench of bodies buried, scores deep, takes a while to get used to. But signs of people living in the crypts prove that, to some, the filth was home. Others came for drugs, or solace and silence, or for a route to the underground. A thick cable stretches over the graveyard, sloping down to the east. A sharply cut tombstone stands astride its fellows, a granite coffee mug bolted to its foundation. The dark marble is speckled with a glimmer of silica. A tombstone apparently built of motorcycle parts occupies a quiet corner.

You can go east (e).

A chill wind blows through your hair.

And while it may look like a desolate and depressing place to be, it also is a very quiet place where one can be outside and not be hassled. It is where I found a little note left by/for Lillith. I found it there shortly after I had learned she had died and in many ways it was of great comfort to me. At some level I felt, hoped maybe, that the message was meant for Eveline, but I think Lillith's player wrote it for her character, her way of saying goodbye. This is what the note said:

It's raining here too, girl
And I guess that's a damn good thing
'Cause no one can tell I'm crying
'Bout the way you used to sing

I remember days stacked onto nights
Where you'd hold me and tell me 'bout pain;
Singing, 'girl, it's all good, bleed all ya want
And don't take no shit 'bout the stain'

It's winter here too, girl
But I ain't all that cold
'Cause I've been drinking a blue streak
But it's getting damn old;

```
I'm getting real tired
And the words are tough to see
Though the world don't have you
You always got me
```

In the same fashion that the world is constantly being re/created, the characters have to be performed. A character that simply stands in a room has a name and a description that the other players can see, but without someone animating the character it might as well not be there. Only through interaction with other characters can one establish an identity for one's character, both outwards for other characters and inwards for the player hirself. In a very key sense, the character's identity is the sum (and then some) of all the character's experiences, interactions and reflections.

The basic techniques of role-playing are really not that difficult. A player has to find hir way around the MUD, primarily using the "go" command, while using the "say," and "emote" commands to interact. After very little practice someone new to mudding can walk around, find someone to talk to and spice up the conversation with a couple of grins, frowns and goatee-scratchings. The hard part is staying true to your character and this is something that one has to learn simply by playing a lot. Even though I as a player may have thought up what kind of character I want to play, I must learn how this character will think, feel, move and act. As my experience as this character grows, it will become easier to switch into the frame of mind that allows this character. This process becomes easier the longer one role-plays, but every new character one plays needs a lot of effort in consciously thinking through how s/he would act in a given circumstance.

The character is thus being formed through the various interactions with other characters and their reactions to the performance of the character. Initially reactions will be based on the name and the description of the character, more than on the actual role-playing. When you get to know a character better, the role-play becomes more and more of a defining factor, because, paradoxical as it sounds in a textual world, actions speak louder than words. The actions, fast paced and thrill filled as a cyberpunk world may be, are for a large part simply the mundane enactments of the character; the way the character coughs before talking to someone, the way someone will always be fiddling with his gun, or the way someone habitually enters a bar and orders a scotch on the rocks. A 28 year old male player, whom I shall call Sayor here, when asked how he acted out idiosyncrasies of his characters, answered:

```
I mostly pay attention to a very detailed description, and
make certain to have a highly developed personality. I try
to keep the personality in mind, using certain key phrases,
```

> phrases and expressions that I [the player] don't use, as though they were by habit. Same with body language. I make sure I have several "hooks" which I can use to remind myself exactly who and what I am playing. In many cases, these "hooks" are very stereotypical.

Habitual behaviors, like Eveline always "brushes some hairs from her cheek, tucking them behind her ear with one fluid motion of her hand and then lets her hand trail down her neck," install a sense of continuity for/in the character. Characters acquire a particular, continuous identity through the re-enactments of certain idiosyncratic behaviors, ways of speaking and dressing, and, of course, ways of reacting and thinking.

In Real Life we assume that someone is the same person we met the other day, simply because s/he is embodied in the same body as last time and speaks and acts in a way largely congruent with the image s/he presented earlier. Only if someone suddenly behaves radically different from the established pattern or shows up in a radically different body (both situations are often "played out" in novels and movies for dramatic effects) do we (have to) start to question the continuity and integratedness of the identity of this person. Online, where we lack the physical access to someone's body, characters depend even more so on the enactments of their bodies and personalities in order to achieve a natural, continuous identity that installs the character as real and believable.

Having "hooks" for your character is important, especially for the performance of gender. "Gender hooks" are often stereotypical, derived from the imagery surrounding men and women in Western societies, in order to get the point across unequivocally. Establishing the right image is especially important when playing a cross-gender character.

> Playing the opposite gender is the ultimate in role-playing challenges. It is much like trying to play another race (elf, dwarf, etc) but is more difficult, in that nobody can actually say "Hey, you're not really an elf!". In other words, not only is it difficult to do, but you can be found out more easily than any other role-playing situation.

Sayor's point is underscored by Graye:

> I think that it's very crucial to attempt to approach situations from the perspective of the gender you're playing, not your own. Being jocular and making cracks back when playing a woman and somebody says "Hey bitch, nice tits. Let's go fuck" makes about as much sense as a man discussing the comfort of different bra makes or men going

to the bathroom in groups; not only does it happen very rarely (giving you away, to a degree), it's also something that's not culturally natural for the given sex to do. If they DO still think you're female after you do something like that, likely as not they'll assing you to a stereotype of female; lesbian, ultrafeminist, bitch, whatever. People are cruel, and playing the opposite sex means thinking like the opposite sex, using the language of the opposite sex (women don't call their breasts jugs or gazungas, nor do men call women's breasts breasts or chest in regular conversation about them (unless they're feeling polite, of course).

A certain hook, such as being teasy (which is usually associated with female characters), allows a player to stay close to hir character, to act and react as hir character would. Playing a teasy girl might for instance lead a player to regularly make suggestive comments as hir character, which in turn reinforces the hook, which in turn allows the player to firmly stay in the frame of mind of hir character. When I asked Shadowschild what, apart from descriptions, was especially important to her when "evaluating" the performance of a character, the following dialogue ensued:

<OOC> Shadowschild says, "Social behaviour. A male character that does not respond when I do this... (look at me)"
Shadowschild poses for you.[36]
Shadowschild smiles at you.
Shadowschild asks, "See anything you like?"
<OOC> Eveline [to Shadowschild]: sure do baby...[37]
<OOC> Shadowschild says, "he is too young or gay or played by a straight female."
Shadowschild grins mischievously.
<OOC> Shadowschild says, "See?"
<OOC> Shadowschild says, "and... when I'm playing around and say..."
Shadowschild [to Eveline]: Know where a girl can get a good big hard sausage?
Shadowschild says, "It's been ages since I've been able to find a good Dulvichney sausage... "
Shadowschild sighs loudly.
Shadowschild grins mischievously.
<OOC> Shadowschild says, "He should respond somehow..."
Shadowschild grins mischievously.
<OOC> Eveline grins

Shadowschild giggles behind her hand.
<OOC> Shadowschild says, "i about killed Storm the other day with that one.... *grin*"
<OOC> Eveline hmms, "does this not have to do more with staying in character than with who plays that character?"
<OOC> Shadowschild says, "Not really..."
<OOC> Shadowschild says, "Hmm... actually... it is both"
<OOC> Shadowschild says, "A really good female player could ride that sort of thing... but when you are roleplaying, you tend to get into character (or I do) and then just react as the character should/does react. If you don't react, yourself... you may not realize the character should have reacted..."

In Shadowschild's last comment the slippage between IC and OOC worlds becomes apparent again. A really good female player may have incorporated her male character's worldview to the point where she will have her character react like a man under all circumstances. The slippage here lies in the telltale "but" trailing that statement. Although you get into character and have your character react as you think it should, "getting in character" does not necessarily mean that you incorporate/adopt a convincing and continuous frame of mind for that character. Especially when playing a cross-gender character, you may not realize that certain character traits and/or behaviors stem from your own RL sensibilities and attitudes, rather than from a logical, continuous, and believably gendered mental construction of that character. But even if you *do* realize it, keeping up the image of a cross-gender character may not be easy, as Dave illustrates:

ahh, well, its kinda hard to come up with source material, since I'm not a woman <grin>, at times I let the male side of me slip, which made her [Dave's female character] turn into more of a tomboy/bitch type thing. it ended up making her really argumentative, and.. well.. unlikable to some. most people figured I was a guy playing a girl from the start <grin> and so I think they treated her more as they'd treat a guy... yeah, I mean, every night it was like 'okay Dave, think girl stuff'. it got really hard especially when talking to OTHER women, cuz I felt like such a fake.[38]

While the slippage here may result in failing to present a convincingly gendered male or female character, the same sort of slippage is essential to role-play other situations convincingly. Graye argues that,

IRL and IC feed off each other.. competing ideas, as it were. it's hard to write or imagine something you've never experienced at all, and it's hard to relate to something you've never done. I think that IRL and IC kind of help you bridge what you've never done with what you've done... maybe incorrectly, but it tries for a connection, shows you what [you] have done (IRL) and what you WOULD do, or wish you COULD do, if you had the chance (IC).

A character may be more or less comprehensively imagined, but for a convincing performance a player must rely on hir own real life experiences, one simply cannot imagine *everything* without having some personal experience to ground the role-play in.

This however does not make playing a cross-gender character convincingly impossible. As I have quoted Kessler and McKenna earlier, "[t]o be successful in one's gender is to prevent any doubt that one's gender is objectively, externally real" (1978: 158). The fundamental doubt with regard to gender online is the fact that the body that is accessible for scrutiny is a consciously constructed body; the player's real body is virtually inaccessible, but that body is nevertheless constructed as ultimate touchstone for the character's performance. A female player playing a male character may be commended on her great RP, but she's still a woman playing the role of a man. The female player's performance is not "objectively, externally real" and hence, as good as she may RP, not successful. Thus there seem to be two options for being successful at playing a cross-gender character. The first is not to reveal any information, or at least no gender-specific information, OOCly to other players. The second is for the player to OOCly pretend to be of the same gender as hir character. A lot of players think that both options are misleading beyond what is permissible. Playing a cross-gender character is considered "good role-playing," but the moment someone mistakes you OOCly for the wrong gender it is not ethical to "lead them on" for one's own "perverted and demented pleasures."

After Shadowschild pointed out the importance of role-playing your character conform the social and game (or theme) related expectations, I asked her if she'd noticed anything particular about how male and female players actually used emotes.

<OOC> Shadowschild thinks...
Shadowschild grins mischievously.
<OOC> Shadowschild says, "Well.. that is one of them, right there.."
<OOC> Shadowschild says, "I have noticed... (in my personal experience) that female players tend to fill in the space... a female [player] will emote just to fill the space while they

type in a more complex thought or say or action.... A male player doesn't... they tend to just emote the 'important' stuff... and leave dead air."
Shadowschild giggles behind her hand.

Not a minute after this conversation took place another character wandered into *The Last Exit.* Shadowschild was anxious to demonstrate what she had just told me and acted out her little performance again. I watched with interest, but Eveline was not much impressed.

Cyric [to Shadowschild]: How're you doin t'night, madam?[39]
Cyric walks over and stands next to Shadowschild.
You gaze out over the crowd, occasionally glancing at Cyric and Shadowschild.[40]
Shadowschild smiles at Cyric. "Quite well, thank you. That is a lovely shirt you have..."
You lean one hand on the bar and start tapping it with your fingernails.
Shadowschild raises an eyebrow at Cyric.
Cyric[41]
Ebon skinned and nearly six feet tall, Cyric is the epitome of intimidating. His dark grey eyes fade from pitch black, to light grey seemingly at will and with a mind of their own. Not a single hair rests on his head, or anywhere else that you can see for that matter. He catches you watching him, and flashes you a crooked smile of sharp teeth covered in gold.
A silk teal dress shirt hangs in billows over his muscular chest and down his arms. Only the highest quality silk was used to make this shirt. Of course you wouldn't expect anything else to be worn by this man. Strapped to Cyric left shoulder is a heavily oiled holster. Covering Cyric's lower body loosely, is a pair of kacki dress pants in near perfect condition, except for the occasional reddish black stain on them. A pair of dress shoes, and black socks adorn his feet, showing off his true personal style.
He is in excellent health.
Cyric is empty-handed.
Cyric looks down at his shirt, "Why thank you" he replies with a slight smirk, "I got this from Bangkok... back when real silk was some where near being affordable.."
Shadowschild says, "Mmm..."

Shadowschild reaches out to lightly touch the shirt. "Teal is one of my favorite colors..."
You stop tapping on the bar and rest your hand on the bar, next to a few empty glasses.
Shadowschild says, "and Thai silk is the best there is.. or so I am told."
Shadowschild poses for Cyric.
Shadowschild [to Cyric]: See anything you like?
Shadowschild grins at Cyric.
[-] *Shadowschild* OOC There he goes... *grin*[42]
Cyric smirks, "Oh, baby.. you do that soo well."
You glance at Cyric and pull up the nearest stool.
[-] *Shadowschild* OOC Male, probably early 20's.. been playing
[-] for a while here... *grin* want to ask him if I'm right?
You sit down on the bar.
[-] Write: 'OOC please do :)' sent to user Shadowschild.[43]
[-] *Shadowschild* OOC *big grin*
Cyric chuckles softly, "quite a bit actually.."[44]
<OOC> Shadowschild says, "Cyric.. can I ask a question?"
<OOC> Cyric says, "sure.."
You shift a little on your stool and lean your back against the bar, your hands resting on your thighs.
<OOC> Shadowschild says, "See.. Eveline and I were having a discussion a little bit ago... and I want to see if my conclusions are correct."
<OOC> Shadowschild says, "Are you male IRL? How old are you? and how long have you been MUDing or MOOing?"
<OOC> You say, "right, blame it on me... *grins*"
<OOC> Cyric says, "yes. 22. and here almost 3 years."
You brush some hairs from your cheek, tucking them behind your ear with one fluid motion of your hand and let your hand trail down your neck.
<OOC> Cyric doesn't MOO/MUD anywhere else.
<OOC> Shadowschild jumps up and down. "Yes! What did I tell you??"
Shadowschild kisses Cyric softly on the lips.
<OOC> Shadowschild says, "Thank you.. .now.. back to the previously scheduled programming..."

Shadowschild again uses a social command, kissing Cyric on the lips, ICly enacting an OOC expression, which she in the following OOC comment immediately qualifies as OOC by saying "back to the previously scheduled programming," meaning "back to IC." While admittedly the emotes and social commands that are used to substitute for body language in text-only virtual environments are often both more affectionate and more violent than IRL (cf. Cherny 1994), it is very interesting to see Shadowschild perform such a "womanly" act as kissing Cyric on the lips out of character. Role-playing is never wholly IC. Even if I as a player am not conversing OOCly with anyone right now, in a crowded room I am bound to see other characters talk OOCly. OOC talk and actions are taken to represent the player hirself and help other players to form an image, however tentative it may be, of that player. Especially in the case of gender these OOC exchanges can provide valuable information. One can imagine that were Lusiphur's player (who for a while also pretended to be a guy OOCly) were to kiss another decidedly male character/player on the lips, whether in IC or OOC fashion, this would raise quite a few eyebrows. `Shadowschild says, "so if the character does not react in the 'expected' fashion.. something is going on. Further encounters will inform you if it is player or character derived."`

Role-playing is thus never wholly objective, nor is it wholly subjective. The player and the character are inseparable and the one cannot be meaningfully read without the other. If a character does not react as expected, it is not automatically taken as an unusual or idiosyncratic reaction of that character, but as a possible indication that the character is acting "falsely," in an out of character fashion that reveals something about the player behind it. In the same way OOC remarks by a player, especially if they seem to indicate that the player may not be of the same gender as hir character, cast doubt on the character's performance. As Fine points out, the fun of the game derives from the fact that player is consciously substituting a fantasy reality for hir everyday reality and that this substituting need not be continuous; it is rather a shifting in and out of, or oscillating between a fantasy reality and everyday reality.[45] The fun, the thrill is imagining oneself as an Other, living in an Other world and dragging the lingering, phosphorescent afterimage of the screen, this feeling of Otherness from the realm of fantasy into the realm of everyday life, savoring the feeling of oneself, one's self as an Other, relishing the possibility of being/becoming an Other.

The performance of the character's body is the focus of some considerable effort. After all, preventing any doubt to arise adds to the believability of the performance and the engrossment in, and construction of the shared, virtual environment. The name and description are important, but rather static parts of the character. They are the basis for the actual performance, the role-playing of the character, and as both Tôsama and Shadowschild have indicated, the role-playing experiences that a player (through hir character) has with another character are added to, layered on or integrated into the mental image that the player has formed. For the player the name and the description of hir character are, in a sense, hooks themselves. Shadowschild rightly says, "`Body language is second most important. That's what separates the good players from the mediocre ones. Instead of just [using the] say [command to express] "whatever", it's so much more inspiring if one uses emotes.`" Not only, I would say, is a good use of emotes inspiring, it is crucial in the construction of the character's body in such a way that both the player hirself and the players with whom s/he interacts can imagine and relate to the character as if s/he were real.

The player must construct an image of the situation, imagine where the characters' bodies are relative to each other and their surroundings in order to evaluate what courses of action are reasonable. The player must not only construct such an understanding for hirself, s/he must construct it cooperatively with the other players involved in the role-playing situation. Fine illustrates this point as follows:

> Frequently the physical location of the characters is the issue – where they stand in relation to other characters. Both referees and players are required to state precisely where the characters are located, and what they and others in the situation are doing. This is not a question of game rules, but is related to the establishment of a consensual game reality. Because characters have no physical presence, the construction of a "reality" is essential. It is a reality without sensory cues, a reality created by talk that is external to the frame. (1983: 108)

Of course, in an online RPG the "talk" that creates the reality is not external to the frame and referees do not control or interfere with the role-playing as such. Precisely because in an online RPG one *acts* as one's character the emotes, the "spoken" references to the surroundings and the other players are integral to the role-playing.[46] Players negotiate the shared fantasy reality of their surroundings mainly by performing their characters' bodies through emotes, in relation to their immediate surroundings and the bodies of the other characters present.

There are two extreme situations where a character's body is extensively played out, namely combat and net.sex. Combat, on Cybersphere, is handled by MOO-code and rarely does one see an emoted fight. When a player has hir character <attack another_character> the combat code takes control; it will decide, through virtual rolls of the dice and the evaluation of the fighting characters' statistics, how, where and how severely the characters "hit" each other. Net.sex, or less crudely, erotic encounters on the other hand show the process by which the character's body is evoked in a less restricted way. In an erotic encounter there is no MOO-code that the player can invoke. Friction, resistance, counter-play and imagination are what evokes the character's body here.

East end of the beach
The somber gray beach terminates here in a gargantuan stone breakwall to the east, running high and long out into the water. Huge waves crash against the breakwall, slowly wearing it down over the endless decades.
Far out to the northeast, in the ocean at the end of the breakwall, you can see the silhouettes of buildings on some kind of peninsula, unreachable from here. The beach extends west for quite a long distance.

Lillith [to Eveline]: Eveline..
Eveline [to Lillith]: Lillith.. swim with me...
Lillith stares at you in slight confusion.
Lillith smiles.
Lillith says, "Yes."
Lillith stands up.
Eveline undoes the zipper of her anthracite latex pants, and strips it down her legs bit by bit making squishy sounds.
Lillith pushes down at the waist of her long lace skirt. It falls with a soft whispering noise to her feet.[47]
You giggle behind your hand.
You stand up.
You take Lillith's hand.v

Lillith carefully drapes her cloak over the katana,[48] attempting to conceal it.
You look at Lillith with a mischievous smile on your face.
Lillith carefully lays her cybermodem on the large heap of collective belongings, and takes your hand.[49]
You giggle at all the stuff on the beach, "now let's run..."
Lillith nods soberly to you.
You dash down the beach towards the surf, water splashing from under your feet as you reach the waterline.[50]
Eveline shouts, "aahhh... cold!"
Lillith stifles a quiet yelp of surprise as the cold water covers her, quickly immersing herself to the neck.
You go under a couple of times and shriek with joy while wiping your hair from your face.
You smile and splash some more, swimming closer to Lillith.
Lillith runs her hands over herself, studying the raised bumps of her body, pushing her short hair from her eyes.
Lillith says, "I can't... swim very well, Eveline."
You wrap your arm around Lillith's waist, kissing her salty lips, "sokay... i'm here... don't go in too deep water."
Lillith

You see a 5'8" female, about 18 or 19, poised on the brink of womanhood. Her dark black hair is cut boyishly short, long bangs hanging in soft feathery tufts around her eyes - pale, smoke- grey, flickering slightly with each change in her environment. Her skin is a deathly pale white, and although rather slender, a well-proportioned figure suggests a graceful body.

Her face has been powdered white. A pentacle has been transposed in heavy black makeup over her face. A small diamond stud glitters in her left nostril. Her long neck is slender and pale, her throat quavering slightly with each breath. A dark black crescent moon is tattooed just above her collarbone. Her bare shoulders are thin and rounded, curving gracefully into her arms. A small, bright silver pentacle rests at the base of her throat, held on a thin chain about her neck. Her arms are long and thin. Slight toning of her upper arms prevent her from appearing bony, and freckles lightly dust the pale white skin. Her hands are a soft white, each long finger ending in a nail painted a glossy black. Bright white scars criscross each wrist just below her palms. Her bare stomach is flat and firm. Ribs are slightly visible on her thin frame, curving sharply in at her waist. Her sex is covered by a small tuft of dark hair, her abdomen sloping gracefully into her upper body. Her bare legs stretch out long and graceful, the muscles slender, but obviously firm and well-toned. Uniformly hairless, the soft skin is a chalk white. Her small feet are pale white. Each toenail is painted a shiny black.

She is in excellent health.

Lillith is empty-handed.

You notice Lillith looking at you.[51]

Eveline

A small and slender, but firmly muscled woman stands before you. Her thick, black hair is cut very short, though it still manages to cover her ears. She has high cheekbones and there might well be running some Asian blood through her veins, even as her complexion is definately Caucasian. Her eyes, ever darting around, are of an emerald green that (again) give her a little bit of an exotic appearance. In general she has a friendly aura about her.

Two bundles of muscles run from just behind her ears along the sides of the neck down to her shoulders, forming at the nape of the neck a sort of a gully. Her shoulders are well developed, showing the twitching and rolling work of the muscles as she moves. A huge tattoo of a Red Tiger covers the biggest part of her back. The Red Tiger's fierce head sits just under her left shoulder blade and is set against an azure backdrop that reminds you of what a scaled dragon is supposed to look like. The tiger's body seems curled up comfortably between her shoulder blades and lower back, its tail curling up over her right shoulder, the black fluffy end resting lazily on her chest, just above her right breast. Judging the lively colors the tattoo must be still quite new. Very dark nipples sit (contently is the word that comes to mind) on her breasts. Though not small her breasts seems smaller in the presence of her firm shoulders. On her left arm, just under her shoulder, sits a little abstract Polynesian tattoo. Its fine lines and little triangles run in a ring around it. On her arms tiny hairs, completely washed white by salt and sun and therefore contrasting with the more bronzed tint of her skin, make her skin there feel very soft. Her fingers are slender but seem to be a bit shorter than average, giving her hands a bit of a 'petite' look. The only part of her body that seems not that muscled is her belly. Just under the round navel it is soft and round, so much so you would give the world to snuggle up and lay your head there. Under a little scar that might as well have had a neon sign saying 'appendix removed', little black curls cover her vagina. Curiously enough her pubic hair is very short without showing any signs of regularly being cut in any way. Her legs again show athleticity, well formed and muscled. Her small left foot features five delightful wiggly toes. And so does her right foot.

She is in excellent health.

Eveline is empty-handed.

Lillith leans into your grasp, using you for support. "When I was a very young girl, I imagined drowning very often.. when I bathed, I would hold my head under water as long as I could, until my body forced me out.."

You hug Lillith closer to you leaving little room for water between our bodies and nod, "strange morbid childhood fantasies... yes..."

Lillith [to Eveline]: What..?

Eveline [to Lillith]: *flatly* i had something like that too... i imagined being cut up into little pieces... *shakes her head* the strange things children think...

Lillith [to Eveline]: Children are very wise. As we age, we forget. We replace that wisdom with something else that we euphemistically call wisdom..

Lillith presses her body against yours, running wet hands down your back.

You shiver at the memories and the cold water, sliding your hands down Lillith's back and onto her buttocks, "forgetting can be very wise too..."

Lillith sighs at your touch, taking her time to compose herself. "Eidetic memories leave one without the option to forget."

You nibble at Lillith's earlobe, "i will not forget this... never..."

Lillith relaxes in your arm, cooing softly.

You stroke Lillith's buttocks and let your hand slide up her side, touching the side of her breasts with your fingertips, your lips kissing their way from her ear down to her shoulder.

Lillith kicks gently in the water, lifting herself a few inches from the sandy bottom, and cranes an arm around your waist to press your upper body against hers.

You turn around your axis, slowly fighting the water's resistance, little eddies forming around us in the water.

You move your hand up and follow Lillith's hairline with your finger, before letting your hand slide down over her shoulder and her back again.

Lillith [to Eveline]: Eveline.. I'm getting very cold.. may we dress?

Lillith slides her body in a slight circular motion against yours, indicating that she enjoys the experience nevertheless.

You nod and wade half swimming back to shallower water with Lillith in your arms, "i'm cold too... and so *grin* tired..."

Lillith smiles happily.

Lillith wades onto shore, and runs a hand over her body, enjoying the sensation of the water evaporating.

You sigh and shake your head vigorously, water spraying around from your hair.

You bend forward and twist your hair between your hands, water dripping on the sand, forming a little puddle.

```
Lillith lets herself drip dry, and bends down, gathering up her
  possessions.
You look up at Lillith and smile warmly.
You take the black Sisters of Mercy T-shirt.
Eveline slips the black Sisters of Mercy T-shirt over her head
  and sticks her arms through the holes that were left by ripping
  out the sleeves and tucks it down over her chest.[52]
Lillith [to Eveline]: That was sudden inspiration, wasn't it,
  Eveline? I could tell by your eyes..
```

Disappointingly maybe, and although probably interesting for analytical purposes, I felt that quoting an all-out net.sex scene is a bit too personal. Nevertheless, I think that the above scene is still a good example of how two players can create their characters' bodies and surroundings through role-playing. Analytically we can distinguish two sorts of emoting in the above example, which I shall call here "self-emoting" and "co-emoting." With self-emoting I mean those actions of a character that do not have any direct effects on another character or the surroundings. With co-emoting I mean those actions of a character that directly, or indirectly through an alteration of the shared surroundings, implicate another character in the action. Since all the role-playing eventually is about co-creating a shared experience, one could say that all emoting is co-emoting. Certain actions however, are more about performing/confirming one's own character in the given situation than that they're about explicitly sharing/co-creating that situation. For instance the way Lillith wades onto shore and runs a hand over her body, or the way Eveline sighs and shakes her head vigorously, or the way Eveline behaves, peripherally, during the little RP situation between Shadowschild and Cyric, these are all emotes where the other character(s) present are not explicitly implicated, nor is the shared context altered in such a way that it affects the other character(s). These emotes *can* of course be taken as a cue for a reaction. Lillith might have emoted getting wet from the water spraying from Eveline's hair or Cyric might have reacted to Eveline tapping her fingernails on the bar.

That's different though, from those emotes where Lillith and Eveline are holding each other, which means that both players must, independently, form a mental representation of the situation. How are our bodies positioned relative to each other? Can I move my left arm up and around her, or is that the arm she's holding on to? How deep is the water and is there a strong current, or, alternatively, is there a lot of room in which we can maneuver, or are we sitting on a small couch? These are important issues because the persistence and "immersivity" of the shared fantasy reality depends on the player's ability to extend that game-reality without overextending it; it's a simultaneous adhering to and extending of the shared context's possibilities. Lillith and Eveline are at the beach and extending the situation with the possibility of swimming in the water, which from a strict MOO-code point of view is not there (although it is mentioned in the description of the "East end of the beach"), is not beyond the scope of the possible. Magically sprouting fins and transforming into a mermaid however is somewhat beyond that scope. Fine notes:

> As with realism, absolute logic is not necessary; what is required is consistency and the belief that the game is logical... [P]layers require this logic, both to incorporate their game selves into the fantasy world – that is, "feel" what the world is like – and also to construct lines of action for their characters with a reasonable presumption of what will happen as a result. Game logic primarily involves a sense of causal consistency – a perceived connection between cause and effect – coupled with the "folk ideas" of the world. (Fine 1983: 83)

The player has to incorporate a model or scheme "representing" the way the virtual world works, in order to be able to "feel" what that world is like. When the player can "feel" what the world is like, what the context does or doesn't allow for, what the form, location and import of the immediate surroundings and the other characters' bodies are, s/he can role-play successfully.

Graye at one point tried to describe what it is like to grasp for that world in the form of text in front of you, a world that seems so real in your imagination, yet at times defies all attempts at translation.

```
[T]he verbs we use on here are kind of like stream-lined
senses: look, inspect, search. streamlined senses...not
really. I meant....more like they're pared down senses?
We're still grasping for images....a picture to fit the
frame of the text we're given, right? in that way, we feel
out other people on the net...through their descriptions,
and through their emotes. [...] we use them to fit together
different parts of the puzzle...look, build, scent,
etc....but they never quite perfectly define things. it's
like we meet people in a fogged room. They write things
down on paper, and we're all deaf. We can't hear them, but
we can read what they write, and hope we can figure out
what their motions mean. but it's impossible to completely
define a person...hence the use of verbs. if we didn't need
that...if we just encountered people as a voice, it'd still
be Graye: Hi there. our heads would do the rest...but they
were never equipped for that. So we've got to fill in the
gaps, and hence the diversity of nudity on the net,
clothing, inspect messages, descriptions, details, and the
```

like. diversity to produce a unified image, breaking things down in parts because we can't transmit the whole experience yet.

The player builds up hir "model" of Cybersphere from the help files on the theme and history of the world, the knowledge of the cyberpunk genre, information gotten through role-playing, but always based on the same general rules of "causal" or maybe "casual" consistency and "folk ideas" that underlay the player's understanding of his RL world.

> Unlike the setting, these "folk ideas" are typically not consciously created by the referee. Rather, the American folk ideas to which these individuals have been socialized are expressed in these fantasy worlds. (Fine 1983: 76)

While the general setting, as laid out in the help files and in the MOO itself, may have been created by the wizards of Cybersphere, again I feel I must underscore the importance of the individual player in the re-creation and continued existence of an online RPG. The folk ideas of "these individuals" are also those of the wizards, but primarily those of the players, which can have some drawbacks, as Graye notes:

[S]omething I always find interesting is how people's interpretations of [Cybersphere] affect their RP and more importantly, their OOC attitude and behaviour. we all see a slightly different theme, and work off a slightly different set of rules. s'why nobody ever agrees on how to RP here, or how to play. Different for everybody. Probably explains why there's such shit IRL, as well.

It may be true that there is a perpetual OOC discussion, to put it mildly, about the exact status and meaning of different elements of the virtual world, but this can be seen as part of the process by which that world is perpetuated. Graye indicates as much when he says that,

I find that meta,[53] the admin/player dichotomy, the RP/PKiller dichotomy,[54] and the IC/OOC dichotomy to be as much an experience as the RP, or the gadgets, which is probably why I stick around for the bullshit... I have FUN with all the bullshit on this game.

Virtual worlds are hardly ever based on a radically different metaphysics. While of course there are "fantastical" elements, some of them inversions of the norm, the basis for the operation of the virtual world is the players' common-sense knowledge of (generally) the Western world.

With regard to the performance of gender, Penumbra perceptively notes that,

[p]eople like to swap roles, but they don't want [to] _redefine_ roles. *nod* Yeah... and in the end, the persona

> that you're playing online is really mostly a projection of your _perceptions_... so maybe all the gender swapping is only serving to _restrict_ people's views instead of broaden them...

I'm not so sure that gender swapping actually restricts people's views on gender, but my discussion of all the strategies for presenting a believably gendered character, all the strategies for preventing other players to doubt the particular presentation of the character, and all the strategies for "reading" the cues with respect to the characters' and the players' gender, seem to confirm Penumbra's observation that most players are not interested in *redefining* gender roles. Most players rather seem interested in establishing "gender knowledge" about other players. Maybe it is exactly the fact that players *do* play cross-gender characters, creating a situation of uncertainty that causes a restriction in the possible behaviors that can still be meaningfully read as either female or male. In order to present a meaningful and 'unquestionable' image players adopt more or less stereotypical feminine or masculine "acts" in their role-play. However we shouldn't forget that the ultimate social anchor of gender, the actual physical body, is not present for scrutiny. This forces players to fragment the presentation of their characters, as Graye notes. Not just the performance has become fragmented, the reading of that performance has too. The character is "written" and "read" through individual cues and partial enactments in a myriad of situations and contexts, and players try to fashion all these fragments into a fantasy whole, animated before the mind's eye.

The inaccessibility of an "objectively, externally, physically" real body means that these fragments ultimately cannot be "grounded," they cannot be checked against a singular, continuous, non-mediated manifestation of the player. The conclusion is that every fragment, every tiny cue and every enactment can be constructed as an indicator of both femininity and masculinity. Even the most stereotypical male or female behavior can be constructed as 'proof' of the fact that the player is playing a cross-gender character, as for instance the explicit sexualization of the character in Maera's case. Only by trying to maintain a certain casual consistency in and between the IC and OOC realms, by skirting the most stereotypical enactments while not losing oneself in too idiosyncratic ones, can a player hope to present an at least superficially convincing character. "If," indeed, as Kessler and McKenna say,

> there are no concrete cues that will always allow one to make the "correct" gender attribution, how is categorizing a person as either female or male accomplished in each case? Our answer... takes the form of a categorizing *schema*. The schema is not dependent on any particular gender cue, nor is it offered as a statement of a rule which people follow like robots. Rather, it is a way of understanding how it is that members of Western reality can see

> someone as either female or male. The schema is: *See someone as female only when you cannot see them as male.* (1978: 158)

Kessler and McKenna's schema reflects the findings of their study of the prevalent "folk ideas" for gender attribution. Especially their finding that in order to "see" someone as male that person needs to sport at least one male gender cue (such as facial hair, chest hair, build, etc.), while the common sense schema says that a person is to be seen as female when they *don't* sport any male attributes (cf. Kessler and McKenna 1978: 158-159), seem to correspond with my own "virtual" experiences. The female gender, as Kessler and McKenna's study shows, is defined by the negation of the male gender, and this schema is very much apparent in online situations.

Online however, the fact that one is dealing with both a character *and* a player complicates the matter. Players read *both* IC and OOC emotes and comments as cues for *both* the player and hir character; the player and hir character are understood to not be performed in a completely detached sense (as the ideal of RP says), but rather the sensibilities and predispositions of the player and the character are understood to influence each other. IC expressions inform the reader about both the character *and* the player, and OOC expressions do so too.

IC and OOC cues are used to form an image of both the character and the player, but the cues are also used to cross-reference the resulting images. There are four "cross-referenced" or "composite" images if we only take the female and male gender into consideration: male player-male character, male player-female character, female player-female character, and female player-male character. The ultimate goal for the player is to "know" the gender of the other player and the schema that guides the player is the same that Kessler and McKenna put forward. The complication lies in the fact that the character's expressions and the player's expressions are individually judged on their "congruency" and "convincingness." But these findings are also continually cross-referenced and the level to which they either confirm or discredit each other is taken as an indicator for which type of (the four above mentioned) character-player hybrid one is dealing with.

> The schema, see someone as female only when you cannot see them as male, is not a statement of positivist fact. It is *not* that "male" gender characteristics are simply more obvious than "female" ones or that the presence of a male cue is more obvious than its absence. The salience of male characteristics is a social construction. We construct gender so that male characteristics are *seen* as more obvious. It could be otherwise, but to see that, one must suspend belief in the external reality of "objective facts". (Kessler and McKenna 1978: 159)

Virtual reality would seem the ideal place to suspend one's belief in the "external reality of objective facts," but the contrary seems to be the case. Players have learned to adjust to the fact that there always remains a sliver of that fundamental doubt. That sliver of doubt however is the reason for all the convoluted strategies that the players employ to attain a possibly false, but persuasive sense of security from the illusion of knowledge of a really real reality behind all the masquerade.

CHAPTER 4

Not an Ethnography

Code

> Kissing in the sunrays I knew that it was Sunday
> 'Cause my memories, like blueprints in my head
>
> —Neneh Cherry, *Somedays*

Studies that explore social phenomena in "virtual" settings, such as (graphical) MUDS, IRC (Internet Relay Chat), mailinglists or Usenet, usually do so by looking at the social exchanges, the social interplay of the participants. The underlying technology is only, if at all, discussed in how it enables or prevents certain exchanges between the participants. The fact that the underlying technology itself is a social construct, that the technology itself already mirrors myriad cultural conceptions is often overlooked.

> I think a lot of the common assumptions we make are actually built-in to the MOO apparatus... The elements of the MOO are constructed for the most part to simulate a real physical community. Ideas like 'privacy' and 'ownership' are constantly implied by the descriptions and properties if not the actual programming of every object. (Ogre as quoted in Whitlock (n.d.))

The MUD-program, the actual software code that enables the players to interact and to consensually create a shared fantasy reality, is the product of the programmer's imagination. The programmer proceeds from an idea of what s/he wants the program to do. In the case of a MUD-program it must simulate an environment mapped along the lines of spatial metaphors that offers a sense of reality, a sense of presence in an actual physical locale, and that offers the "tools" for meaningful social interaction. The programmer then, proceeds from hir common sense understanding of what it means to "be" in a particular place and "converse" with another person. The outcome is a program based on the programmer's common sense understanding of how "the world" works and how the text-only abstraction of the code can still meaningfully represent the players and offer them meaningful avenues for interaction.

The easiest abstractable form of communication, speaking, is usually implemented in several different commands that reflect the different ways of speaking IRL. You can, for example, "say" something and everybody in the same room will be able to "hear" it; you can also "whisper" to a particular character and only that character/player will be able to hear you, while others in the room can "see" that you are whispering, but cannot hear what you're saying; you can also use "directed speech" that shows everybody who is present to which person specifically you are speaking; you can also "shout," making sure that even characters in adjoining rooms will hear what you have to say. Another example is the way descriptions are implemented on different MUDs, which shows that it is important to also consider the role that the software plays in enabling and defining how the virtual world, and hence the character and its "virtual" gender, can be "build" or "performed."

> After listening to these normative 'whispers' from the machine again and again, I don't think it is uncommon to be upset by lapses or intrusions in the MOO's (however illusory) physical laws. These are reflected in the decrying by players and wizards alike of spoofing,[55] spying, spamming[56] and system hacking. The assumptions have already been made. (Ogre as quoted in Whitlock (n.d.))

As Ogre indicates, whether good or bad, the system (the MUD) that has been implemented to enable the virtual world and its inhabitants "embodies" a set of norms, the virtual version of natural law, if you will.

The norms embedded, or rather, encoded in the MUD-code derive from our everyday reality. The MUD-code is thus not a neutral piece of code, but a culturally, politically and linguistically informed program that enables players to perform certain desired acts. With "act" here I mean that the programmers of the MUD-code proceeded from a particular idea(l) of social interaction and by programming certain routines make possible, from a software point of view, such "acts" as creating a character, naming and describing it, and emoting and speaking for that character.[57]

In his article *Living Inside the (Operating) System: Community in Virtual Reality* John Unsworth details how Unix (the operating system that runs most internet-servers) and MOO-code reflect/encode the cultural and institutional beliefs of the people and the institutions that spawned them.

> [M]OO's in general take shape under twin forces not unlike fate and free will, where free will is what we always have understood it to be, but where the role of fate is played by the operating system in which the MOO is embedded. The aporia in this analogy, and it is an important one for my argument, is that unlike transcendental fate, computer operating systems are historically and culturally determined. (Unsworth n.d.: n.p.)

Unix is that operating system in which MOOs are embedded. It was developed by AT&T's Bell Labs during the 1960s and 1970s to offer multiple users simultaneous access to then very expensive mainframe computers.

> The Unix filesystem is hierarchical in its organization, and the particular kind of hierarchy is, in essence, dendritic: file systems have a tree-like structure, with a "root" directory containing files and other directories, or branches, of the filesystem, which in turn can contain other files and directories. In Unix, every file (and indeed, every process) has an individual owner, and the hierarchy of owners explicitly mirrors the hierarchy of the filesystem itself, with the superuser of all users and user groups called "root." (Unsworth n.d.: n.p.)

Unsworth mentions several factors that were of crucial importance for the development of Unix. Bell Labs received a relatively large amount of money for research from AT&T, the former telecom monopolist, which gave researchers quite some leeway on their projects, but working for a commercial company a certain amount of research was still expected to "pay off". AT&T, mindful of the then recently settled anti-trust lawsuits, decided to distribute Unix at or near cost to universities while setting a prohibitively high price for other companies. That meant that AT&T offered next to no support, which in turn lead to the formation of an informal, cooperative support system in which the users helped each other. These factors, combined with the fact that Unix was designed with communication and the sharing of precious mainframe resources in mind, led to an operating system that incorporated both the institutional, hierarchical qualities "ordained" by the company where it was developed *and* the individual, but cooperative and communicative qualities of the programmers who made it.

> On the one hand, as a mental representation of the universe of information, Unix is deeply indebted to culturally determined notions such as private property, class membership, and hierarchies of power and effectivity. [...] On the other hand, this tool, shaped though it was by the notions of ownership and exclusivity, spawned a culture of cooperation, of homemade code, of user-contributed modifications and improvements... in short, of "fellowship." (Unsworth n.d.: n.p.)

MOO-code was developed at Xerox Parc, also in a well-funded research facility where researchers could "get away" with doing some research that didn't have any immediate commercial applications.[58] MOO-code runs, first and foremost, on Unix machines and Unsworth details how the MOO-code and Unix share quite a few characteristics. A MOO too is a hierarchical system, where the users (wizards, programmers, players) have tightly controlled access to the MOO's objects, depending on the permissions detailed by their hierarchical status. The objects, the building blocks that form the very fabric of the MOO, are themselves ordered in a hierarchical fashion; different orders of objects relate to each other in a parent-child (directory and file) system and the first object (#0) from which the moo universe proceeds can be likened to the Unix "root-directory". Most importantly, Unsworth says, both Unix and the MOO are "command interpreters" and programming environments, and both are "user extensible" from within.[59]

> The important difference between a MOO and the Unix operating system, though, is that while both may be considered to be mental representations, or self-representations, of information processing – models, if you will, of collective memory, of communal libraries, even of collective intelligence – the MOO is the world it models, as well as the model of that world. In other words, if capitalism is a first-order model of the way labor and value and power circulate in the world, Unix is a second-order simulacrum of the way that a particular kind of capital, namely information, works in the world, and the MOO – an inhabitable model of Unix – is then a third-order simulacrum of the world, in which information is not only a representation of labor, and a source of power, and a form of value, but is also quite literally the form that the species-being takes, "not unreal, but a simulacrum, never again exchanging for what is real, but exchanging in itself, in an uninterrupted circuit without reference or circumference."[60] (Unsworth n.d.: n.p.)

The way that the MOO-program, that "third-order simulacrum," has taken form very much resembles Fine's description of how a referee forms hir own fantasy reality based on, for instance, the AD&D sourcebook.

> Referees systematically transform historical or current events to produce the fantastic world, extrapolating from contemporary social problems, politics, and human nature. These fantasies do not emerge spontaneously, but are culturally conditioned, although sophistication in setting construction produces a world unrecognizable to an outsider. (Fine 1983: 75)

The referee and the wizard draw from the AD&D sourcebook and Unix, that have laid down the ground rules, but the sourcebook and Unix themselves are already predicated on the cultural and institutional context that spawned them. On top of that the referee and the wizard build their own culturally conditioned virtual world by extrapolating from contemporary social problems, politics, and human nature.

Gender is one of the preconceptions on which the MOO is constructed. Every object in the MOO that represents a character (or a non-player character) must have a gender. Having a gender is a requisite for characters, even if it's set to a "neutral" gender such as "neuter" or "spivak," simply because the MOO uses pronouns throughout to refer to the character-object. Because of the MOO's requirement that a character must have a gender there is no such thing as a truly genderless character: even a gender neutral character will have to feature a "neutral" gender with its own set of pronouns.[61]

The pronouns that the MOO uses internally are actually "pronoun-substitutes," variables that the MOO-program will fill in depending on the gender of the character-object requiring them. This is done so as to make a single description amenable to all genders. For instance, when a character puts on a shirt, the MOO must display a message informing the player who puts it on and all the other characters present of what happens. The MOO however, does not know on forehand who will wear that shirt, so if Eveline were to put on a shirt with a message on it that reads, "%N pulls the shirt over %p head and admires %r in the mirror", it would be rendered by the MOO for Eveline's female gender as, "Eveline pulls the shirt over her head and admires herself in the mirror", whereas for a spivak the MOO would gen(d)erate, "Spivak pulls the shirt over eir head and admires eirself in the mirror."[62]

In Cybersphere the character's gender is set in "character generation" and is not freely changeable as in most other (social) MOOs, unless the character uses the services of a "Mod-shop" where for a price a new appearance and even a new sex can be had. The gender of the character is thus fairly stable once it is set. During the time I played on Cybersphere I have only witnessed one character *as a character* change hir gender. The pronouns are used consistently in virtually every message throughout the MOO to refer to the character. The player hirself and the other players are thus constantly reminded of the character's gender. Even, for instance, were I to leave all pronouns and other gender references such as "guy" or "woman" out of my description, the MOO would still append the appropriate pronoun in the message "She is in excellent health" whenever someone decides to look at my character's description. If I wish to use the pose command and enter <.scratch my head>, the "my" will be substituted by the correct pronoun, so that another player would see "Eveline scratches her head." The character is thus always gendered.

In fact, it would seem that the gender of the character is just as visible (if not more) as IRL. The gender of the character may at first be taken at face value; after all, you have to start somewhere as a player, and it might as well be here, with trusting this other player. The fact is however, that with "appropriating" the gender the character also "appropriates" the whole cultural consensus on that gender and whether the player thinks this is right or wrong, the character is expected to behave properly. Behaving "properly" however, is impossible. There appears to be no single "condition for failure," nor would there appear to be a single "condition for success." The same sort of behavior will in one situation by one player be taken as a confirmation of one's gender, while another player might take it as a negation of one's gender. This not only goes for cross-gender characters, but for all characters. Although not a fool-proof method, the only way in which a character stands some kind of chance of being "convincing" is for the player to insist that IRL s/he is of the same gender as hir character (and, obviously, the player should then refrain from making such obvious mistakes as using gender incongruous pronouns).

But gender IRL, as Kessler and McKenna and Butler argue, suffers from the same fundamental uncertainty. The sheer ubiquity and social compellingness of the attribution process of gender obscures the fact that "naming" someone a woman or a man attributes to that person an "objectively and externally real" physical body. A physical body whose objective and external realness is a necessary discursive construction that forms the social legitimization for gender and genderdifferences. A physical body whose very materiality is not questioned, but that is only "readable," only meaningful in terms of the discourse that constructs it as objectively and externally real. A discourse that, as Foucault (1975) and Butler (1993) argue, is legitimized by a particular discipline of the bodies that embody and perpetuate it. A discourse that is predicated on the "unspeakable" (Tyler 1987; 1993) and the "abject" body (Butler 1993: 2-3, et passim). The "unspeakable" and the "abject" however, by being excluded, by being the defining "Other" to the "speakable" and the "virtuous," are at the heart of what constitutes the discourse. A discourse that will discipline the body into renouncing an abject position "outside" of the discourse, where the body is meaningful only in a negation of the discourse's discipline. Not just the abject body, but every/body conforming to this discourse that is grounded in exclusion and abjection embodies the unspeakable, the abject. And every/body runs the risk of being sniffed out and expelled, if not snuffed out. Acting as if nothing is the matter, preventing any doubt that it is not "objectively and externally real," making sure there is no "single condition of failure," in short performing/ propagating/perpetrating the discourse as it is taught is the body's only option.[63]

Bad Form II

I conform
make do with form
I fit in
fit in being busy

Smiling
a necessity
The body
impure

Hidden in my skin
the writing on the wall
Outside's insides
nonconformity's signs

I read
but not what you wrote
I write but not
my skin, myself

Eveline Edz, *Bad Form II*

The MOO mirrors the regime of the body both in its code and in the expected code of conduct. And although "virtual reality" seems to offer an escape from the objectively and externally real body by letting the player construct a virtual counterpart and offering a choice of non-conventional genders for it, a "true" escape in the form of preserving one's anonymity and refusing to give any information about one's "real life" gender comes at the cost of other players' disgruntlement and ultimately rejection. For about a year a player, whom I respect very much for his role-playing, and I had been interacting almost entirely ICly. When we finally got to talk OOCly, the conversation eventually turned to gender. In my recalcitrance of having to consider gender at every step of the way, I gave him the runaround for the best part of an hour, now implying that I might be female IRL, then implying that I might be male. He didn't take no for an answer and eventually he got rather annoyed with the whole conversation.

> Ah, yet more word tangling. Obviously, the whole subject of 'Gender' was a bad one, yet you still failed to answer my question directly. You have thrown quite the vast curves for questions, yet nothing precise. See, I'm a straight to the point type of guy, I ask a question, I normally get a straight, definite answer back and I like things that way. When I have to analyze things, I do, though I attempt to avoid that since I work in the computer industry and all I do is analyze one thing or another all day every day. In your statements, you could be a Female, RL. Or, a male that feels as though he is a 'female trapped in a male's body' or Sexually challenged as some would say, or Homosexual as us rude Americans would call it. [...] Riddles and word twisting, annoy me to no end after a time, so be careful with continuing this 'variety' you are pursuing. As per what [kind of image of you] I had [formed in my] mind, hrm, that matters little. All that is focused on my mind right now, is just how bloody annoyed I am slowly becoming. As per the 'definite' answer, it matters little now, since I am slowly becoming disinterested.

Eventually I told him I was a guy IRL. I don't think, as he said, it mattered anymore. We never really spoke again, nor did we RP beyond the obligatory public greetings.

The Real Body

I don't exist when you don't see me
I don't exist when you're not here
What the eye don't see won't break the heart
You can make believe when we're apart
But when you leave I disappear

—The Sisters of Mercy, *When you don't see me*

Words are the chief means by which worlds are created and sustained.

—Stephen Tyler, *Vile Bodies – A Mental Machination*

The material presented and the analysis so far might seem to be, well, almost hell-bent on refuting the claims of virtually every researcher of gender online that "cyberspace," and MUDs in particular, finally offer a space where "[g]ender is divorced from the body..." (Reid 1994: n.p.). Online it would seem players can play cross-gender characters or even choose a non-conventional gender and cyberspace thus is a space that offers the possibility of subverting the notions of gender. If anything, it would seem, I have been reinstating, if not essentializing gender, gender-roles and even the body, although I hope to have also shown that if the body is essentialized it is always a discursively essentialized body, a body installed as essential by a discourse that seeks legitimization therein.

Karin Spaink warns that if you look for differences in gender behavior and start with categorizing your subjects along the lines of their "natural," "biological" sex, male and female, then you *will* find differences (1998: 19). Not only will you find differences, generally the paradigm of the differentiated, "objectively and externally real" body is so great that the gender dichotomy is re - inscribed with force. If even my invocation of Butler and Kessler and McKenna could not prevent this from happening, then the question looms large... What happened? Tomasz Mazur asks the same sort of question when he says that,

> [v]irtually all critical works on gender in MUDs as of today base their examination of gender in virtual space on the real vs. virtual dichotomy. There is the world of the MUDs, where individuals interact, morph or gender-swap but there is always the body at the computer keyboard, fixed and "real." Why is the "real" of the gendered body never questioned? (1994: n.p.)

In order to question the "real" of the gendered body, Mazur then harks back to the conception of cyberspace as an "other" space, saying that,

> [w]hat the critical discourse on sex and gender in the virtual space requires is to get beyond a mere discussion of gender stereotypes and of how "real"

> gender is reproduced or "subverted" virtually. Virtual environments offer a space for the examination of the concepts of identity, subjectivity and representation which should be recognized and employed in the search of a theory of difference which can "work out" the gendered body without relying on the real/virtual binarism and, ultimately, essentializing the body. (1994: n.p.)

Mazur might not agree here with the fact that I think that he thinks that cyberspace is *still* an "other" space. I will return to this matter presently. Earlier Mazur invokes Baudrillard's (in)famous Disneyland example —

> Disneyland is there to conceal the fact that it is the "real" country, all of "real" America, which *is* Disneyland... Disneyland is presented as imaginary in order to make us believe that the rest is real, when in fact all of Los Angeles and the America surrounding it are no longer real, but of the order of the hyperreal and of simulation. (Baudrillard 1983: 25)

— to argue that,

> [B]audrillard's theory of simulations does not help in establishing a clear definition of the virtual; quite the opposite: it clearly shows that the real, which serves as a basis for defining the virtual, is just as ambiguous and unstable. The construction of a cyberbody, then, takes place in a space quite similar to that of the "real" body: a "real" which is a simulation rather than reality. This further problematizes the real/virtual dichotomy, suggesting that both the real and the virtual are simulations. (Mazur 1994: n.p.)

Indeed, Baudrillard argues that the "real is no longer real" (1983: 25). More so even, the "real" is a simulacrum for which there is no original. "Virtual Realities" and simulations such as Disneyland only serve the "reality principle" (Baudrillard 1983: 25; cf. Mitchell 1989: 222) and conceal the fact that they do not simulate a really real reality in fantasy, but that they simulate a fantasy reality in a reality fantasy (cf. Tyler 1987: 216). This is the same compelling obscurantist principle at work, as Butler tells us, that obfuscates the installation of a "natural," continuous gender identity and an "essential" body through the performance of gender.

The "real" did not disappear recently, when Baudrillard visited Disneyland. It did not disappear when Ferdinand de Saussure (1916) argued that the signifier's signifieds were concepts, mental images and not actual objects. Even earlier, in the late nineteenth century, the "real" had already disappeared as Timothy Mitchell argues. When Egyptian scientists visited the World Exhibition of 1889 in Paris, on their way to the Eighth International Congress of Orientalism in Stockholm, they were confronted with a spectacle where

> [e]verything seemed to be set up as though it were the model or the picture of something, arranged before an observing subject into a system of signifi-

> cation, declaring itself to be a mere object, a mere "signifier of" something further. (Mitchell 1989: 222)

The Egyptian scientists were, for example, confronted with a street, carefully fashioned to resemble as closely as possible a "real" street of medieval Cairo, so life-like that "even the paint on the buildings was made dirty" (ibid.: 217). When they thought they'd enter a mosque, they however discovered that it was a facade, hiding, to their embarrassment, "a coffee house, where Egyptian girls performed dances with young males, and dervishes whirled" (ibid.: 217). Venturing outside of the exhibition the visitors learned that,

> [t]he machinery of representation was not confined to the exhibition... Almost everywhere that [the] Middle Eastern visitors went, they seemed to encounter this rendering up of the world as a thing to be viewed. (ibid.: 221)

The zoo and the public gardens offered up flora and fauna for the scrutinizing gaze, but the countryside was also carefully groomed by and ordered for the (then) new agri*cultural* machinery and cultivation methods. Even the Alps had become a spectacularly organized "view" from a railway carriage, gliding along a track laid out to maximize the vistas suddenly coming into view when rounding yet another bend, or exiting yet another tunnel (ibid.: 221-222).

> Characteristic of the Europeans' way of life was their preoccupation with what an Egyptian author described as *intizam al-manzar,* the organization of the view. Outside the world exhibition, it follows paradoxically, one encountered not the real world, but only further models and representations of the real. (ibid.: 221)

Mazur then, following Baudrillard's somewhat 'ecstatically' worded theory, equates the "real" and the "virtual" in that both are "simulations,"[64] which leads him to say that,

> [t]he examination of gender construction in the virtual space of MUDs, then, should offer an insight into the concepts of gender identity without insistence on a "real," stable and fixed body. It should also result in the collapsing of the real/virtual dichotomy. (Mazur 1994: n.p.)

Indeed, my research has been based, albeit more or less implicitly, on the assumption that finding out how gender "works" online would offer some insight in how gender "works" offline, in "real life." This assumption however recreates the difference between "virtual" and "real" again. Still, the resulting material managed to collapse the "real/virtual dichotomy," but maybe not quite as Mazur would have expected. Instead of "elevating" the status of gender to the level of the simulacrum, the performance of gender online is "dragged down" to the level of the (assumed) objectively and externally real body. This body is not "the real body," for that body is "unspeakable," "illegible;" it does not exist. It is the fiction of the Real Body that collapses the real/virtual dichotomy.

The question then, why cyberspace is an "other" space in Mazur's line of argument, can be answered by considering that, even though he wants to collapse "the real/virtual dichotomy", the "virtual" in his argument functions as a site, an origin of contestation for the "real". For the "real" to be collapsed by the "virtual," the virtual must undermine the real. The virtual thus must be an "other" space that subverts (or maybe perverts) the fantastic idea that the real is the really Real and not a simulacrum, and thus the two should collapse in a phantasmagoria of imaginaries. The "really Real" however has been quite fantastic for a long while and by spinning off ever more fantastic "virtual realities," or "other spaces" it keeps concealing that. In fact, most of us are willing, if maybe somewhat ignorant, accomplices to its "reality effects."

It might be interesting to further discuss the real, the virtual and their relations, but I don't think that I can resolve the problems surrounding the ontological status of the virtual, let alone the ontological status of the real. For all intents and purposes the "real," even if we choose to construct it as a construction, is the reality we actually live in. Fantasy or not, it's the world whose rules we must ultimately obey, for it is this common sense, everyday world that holds power over our bodies. My body, whether I consider it a construction, a natural biological example of my species, or some god's creation, is the body that can and will be punished, disciplined or killed. Reality is my common sense context and

> [i]ndividuals, constituted as subjects and objects within a particular framework, are produced by that process into relations of power. An individual can become powerful or powerless depending on the terms in which her/his subjectivity is constituted. (Walkerdine in Blackman 1998: 144)

Maybe the difference that Mazur tries to overcome lies in the ultimate accountability of the body. In everyday reality the body can be held "physically" accountable. In virtual reality the virtual body may be punished too (or even "erased", cf. Dibbell (1993)) and while the "punishment" of the virtual body may be a psychological blow to the RL player of that virtual body, it is not a physical blow.[65]

Instead then, of trying to doggedly define what cyberspace *is,* there is another way to understand, to conceptualize the "reality gap," that strange lapse of reality that cyberspace presents us with. One of the most defining characteristics of cyberspace is its ephemeral quality. Cyberspace and the MUD are consciously entered by dialing in and logging on, "there" for the time being, but "gone" when the connection is. Virtually every researcher of cyberspace picks up on the fact that once you are "online" you have "entered another realm," where things work just a bit differently and where you are, or can become someone else to a degree. The "online experience" is often described by metaphors of travelling through unknown territory, from which you eventually return to tell your friends about the experience or maybe to write a travelogue (Dibbell 1998; Markham 1998). When discussing cyberspace more theoretically it becomes an "in-between" or a "contested" space (Mazur 1994) and Sherry Turkle aptly calls it a "transitional space" (1995: 263). At the heart of the "otherness" of cyberspace and the metaphors of travelling, lies the largely implicit understanding that the experience of cyberspace is (or can be) transformational. Transformation not on a grand, dramatic scale, although that is a possibility too, but mostly on the mundane level of reflexivity, a bit of a heightened self-consciousness, if only because of the fact that in e-mail you tend to say things that you wouldn't say, or wouldn't phrase as directly, IRL, face-to-face.

MUDs, and role-playing MUDs in particular, offer a very conducive setting for a transformational experience. If we don't consider the MUD so much as a "place", a contested concept in cyberspace anyway, but rather as an episodic event in the player's life, then the nature of the transformational aspect becomes more clear. The time that the player spends "in-between", in limbo, *in* the MUD can be likened to the liminal period of *rites de passage.* The analogy between the MUD and the liminal phase offers a theoretical approach that provides insight in the experience of cyberspace and its "function" within role-playing. Therefore I want to consider online role-playing in the light of Victor Turner's discussion of liminality.

A *rite de passage* is a "ritual of passing"; it is a religious or secular ritual that expresses, makes possible, and itself *is* the passing of a subject from one state or position in life to another. Here we can think of such rituals as both religious and secular marriage, circumcision, attaining adulthood/manhood/womanhood, being installed into religious or secular office, or receiving one's Master's degree.

> Van Gennep [who is identified with the phenomenon because of his 1909 book about rites of passage] himself defined "*rites de passage*" as "rites which accompany every change of place, state, social position and age." [...] Van Gennep has shown that all rites of transition are marked by three phases: separation, margin (or *limen*), and aggregation. (Turner 1964: 94, italics in original)

In his text Turner especially focuses on the liminal period of the rituals of passage, and thus he pays particular attention to those

> *[r]ites de passage* that tend to have well-developed liminal periods. On the whole, initiation rites, whether into social maturity or cult membership, best exemplify transition, since they have well-marked and protracted marginal or liminal phases. (ibid.: 95)

I don't want to liken playing on a MUD to some sort of occult ritual, nor do I wish to imply that it is any sort of ritual as such. In his monograph Fine delves deep into how the game is played, how entire worlds, societies and cultures are fashioned from fantasy, rulebooks and common sense knowledge, and how the role-playing subculture works, but overall he says that the "fun" element of playing the game is the prime motivator for the players (1983: xii, 233). I feel that it is important here to underscore that role-playing in the first place is a game and that the fun of playing is the prime motivation for most players. The reason then that I am calling on Turner (and Van Gennep) is that there are several striking parallels between the more abstract meaning and functioning of rituals of passage and role-playing in a MUD. By calling on the insights developed with regard to the characteristics and qualities of the liminal period I hope to illuminate certain aspects of the online role-playing experience, especially the "transformational" aspect and the importance placed on the body.

A ritual of passage, as Turner indicates, is divided into three parts: separation, liminal period, aggregation. In, for example, an initiation ritual the "neophytes" are generally separated from the rest of their society, literally by seclusion or metaphorically by special clothing or adornments. The liminal period can generally be characterized as a learning period; whatever the neophyte is being initiated in, s/he must learn the rules for it. Since the initiation ritual marks a transition between a former and a new phase or state in the life of the neophytes, during the liminal phase they are "in-between." Turner remarks that, "[t]he symbolism attached to and surrounding the liminal *persona* is complex and bizarre" (1964: 96, italics in original). The neophytes have no standing or attributes and they are oft metaphorically defined by symbols "[d]rawn from the biology of death, decomposition, catabolism, and other physical processes that have a negative tinge, such as menstruation..." (ibid.: 96). The lack of a place in the social structure is mirrored by the dissolution of a frame of reference for the neophytes, they themselves have become unclassified and unclassifiable.

> The neophytes are sometimes said to "be in another place." They have physical but not social "reality," hence they have to be hidden, since it is a paradox, a scandal, to see what ought not to be there! Where they are not removed to a sacred place of concealment they are often disguised, in masks or grotesque costumes... (ibid.: 98)

The liminal period is also a learning phase that prepares the neophyte for hir new role or state. Neophytes can learn individually and introspectively, as in a Vision Quest (ibid.: 100) or they can be taught/instructed. If the neophytes are instructed "[t]he authority of the elders is absolute, because it represents the absolute, the axiomatic values of society in which are expressed the 'common good' and the common interest" (ibid.: 100). While in the relationship between the neophytes and their instructors the latter have absolute authority, the relationships between the neophytes themselves are characterized by absolute equality. So during the times they are not being instructed, the neophytes

> [c]an "be themselves," it is frequently said, when they are not acting institutionalized roles. Roles, too, carry responsibilities and in the liminal situation the main burden of responsibility is borne by the elders, leaving the neophytes free to develop interpersonal relationships as they will. They confront one another, as it were, integrally and not in compartmentalized fashion as actors of roles. (ibid.: 101)

The teaching, as Turner explains, often takes place through "object" lessons. The neophytes are immersed in a situation divorced from everyday reality and are taught the *sacra* (ibid.: 102), the essential ideas and knowledge that give meaning to the neophytes' transition and mark their passing, often by means of performances or chants characterized by grotesque masks, costumes or figurines, displaying exaggeratedly big or small heads, ears, noses, genitals and/or other culturally meaningful characteristics. Because the neophytes are divorced from everyday reality and because they are confronted with the elements of that everyday reality in disproportionate forms,

> [l]iminality may be partly described as a stage of reflection. In it those ideas, sentiments, and facts that had been hitherto for the neophytes bound up in configurations and accepted unthinkingly are, as it were, resolved into their constituents. These constituents are isolated and made into objects of reflection for the neophytes by such processes as componental exaggeration and dissociation by varying concomitants. (ibid.: 105)

Eventually, all the "[u]ndoing, dissolution, decomposition are accompanied by processes of growth, transformation, and the reformulation of old elements in new patterns" (ibid: 99) and the neophytes "are shown that ways of acting and thinking alternative to those laid down by the deities or ancestors are ultimately unworkable and may have disastrous consequences" (ibid.: 106).

The ritual of passage is thus a metaphorical journey that transposes its subject from one "state" to another. It does so by "stripping the subject bare," immersing hir in an environment where "the rules don't apply" and offering hir the opportunity to reflect on the state of things in the everyday world from "outside" its frame, often from an "abject" position. It is important here, to make a distinction between a situation where "there are no rules" and the liminal period. During the liminal period it's not that there are no rules, rather the liminal period is an institutionalized way to "suspend" the rules, to imagine alternatives, but only as a "fiction," embedded in the knowledge that a return to the everyday reality also means a return to the only correct set of rules.

The parallels with the MUD should be becoming clear now. The MUD too is a metaphorical space or period "in-between," that is to be entered and exited again. The player makes a network connection and logs/travels into the MUD and the character "awakes." Eventually the player also leaves the MUD again by logging out and the character generally "goes to sleep." The player, upon entering a new MUD or starting a new character, starts with a blank slate and has to create hir character from scratch. The character is often constructed in a highly symbolic (Lillith's wrists), complex (the way a nickname can hide the character's real name, which in turn is an important aspect of that character's personality) and/or bizarre ways (FurryMUCK's anthropo-beasty-morphs). Real life status and qualities don't apply, every player is only as good as hir performance.

Cybersphere, because it offers a relatively realistic world, extrapolated from our current world to some relatively near future, relies quite heavily on an adequate rendering of "reality" to offer an engrossing role-playing environment. The common sense rules that define Cybersphere's reality are largely derived from everyday western reality, yet those rules are "suspended," in the sense that the player can pick and choose what to use, what not to use and what to invert/convert/subvert in the creation and playing of hir character as s/he sees fit.

> [I]n some respects, I think CS is an excellent reflection of RL. it's what people WANT to be manifested, in a place that they think that the world is going. kinda like two oppositions; Cybersphere is the setting of all the despair people have for the future, and yet it's the resting place of all their hopes. They try to be what suits them best... the most realized aspects of the archetypes they secretly admire. nobody plays a character they have contempt for, or don't enjoy except, perhaps, as a personal experiment, or to support a plot, but longterm characters always seem to be reflections of a person's Fantasy. What would I do, had I power to do this? who would I be, had I influence? it's kind of like online communities... like CS... are distilled versions of RL, peppered with a lot of creative interest. an interpretation of what IS, as much as we understand, thrown in with what might BE.

Graye's comment illustrates the reflexive nature of the MUD. The players are confronted with a world where the everyday rules don't quite apply, but that in a key sense does reflect their everyday world. The players are challenged to explore the possibilities and alternatives that the MUD offers to the problems they encounter. The MUD offers a space that is "in-between" reality and fantasy; ideally it is a "place" that is real enough to offer culturally meaningful responses to the players' behavioral experiments, but unreal enough that it doesn't (have to) impose discipline and punishment on "unaccepted" behavior. The discussion of gender, but this also goes for "virtual" violence, shows that the MUD is not a lawless place, and gender and violence *are* bound by rules.

> Since these games involve fantasy – content divorced from everyday experience – it might be assumed that *anything* is possible... Since fantasy is the free play of a creative imagination, the limits of fantasy should be as broad as the limits of one's mind. This is not the case, as each fantasy world is a fairly tight transformation by the players of their mundane, shared realities. While players can, in theory, create anything, they in fact create only those things that are engrossing and emotionally satisfying. Fantasy is constrained by the social expectations of players and of their world. (Fine 1983: 3, italics in original)

The "suspension" of the rules doesn't offer total and unrestrained freedom, but it allows the player to "play" with the rules and by evaluating the reactions s/he gets, so s/he learns how the rules "work" and how s/he can apply them to achieve what s/he wants.

In real life gender is a crucial, culturally determined social organizer that by and large is immutable.

> As members of society, most of us see only what we expect to see, and what we expect to see is what we are conditioned to see when we have learned the definitions and classifications of our culture. A society's secular definitions do not allow for the existence of a not-boy-not-man, which is what a novice in a male puberty rite is (if he can be said to be anything). (Turner 1967: 95)

Online gender 'suddenly' becomes uprooted and is one of the primary targets for experimentation.

> If the liminal period is seen as an interstructural phase in social dynamics, the symbolism both of androgyny and sexlessness immediately becomes intelligible in sociological terms without the need to import psychological (and especially depth-psychological) explanations. Since sex distinctions are important components of structural status, in a structureless realm they do not apply. (Turner 1967: 98)

For the *player* the MUD is a "structureless realm" because hir everyday reality and its common sense rules have been bracketed, suspended by the fantasy reality of the game and neither do the rules of the everyday MUD-reality apply to the player. For the *character* however the MUD is *not* a "structureless realm." The character lives in a world that is supposed to be real for hir and thus s/he has to comply with its rules. The player however, being momentarily freed from hir social constraints, can pick and choose how to perform hir character and can play with the rules. This also explains the players' interest in another player's RL gender. The gender of the character is something relatively straightforward: the gender for the character is set and easily accessible, and usually the character displays an explicitly female or male description. The character after all is not in a liminal phase, the player is. The player is not here nor there, hir body is parked in front of the screen while hir consciousness dwells in an "other" place. S/he is "in-between," essentially in a structureless realm, unclassified and ultimately unclassifiable.

Experimentation with gender does not necessarily have to take the form of gender swapping. Instead of playing a cross-gender character a player can also experiment with the personality of the character, making the character "more masculine" or "more feminine" by changing aspects of the character that relate to its gender. A 20 year old male player said,

> [i]t's just a matter of acting -- you visualise a person to model yourself after -- either someone imaginary or someone you know IRL, try to get inside their head, and let your intuition take over. It's most effective, I think, if you don't actually change your basic personality too much -- just "feminise" or "masculinise" it.

It may of course be a bit of a blow to the player's ego if hir experiment goes really wrong and the character is a hopeless caricature, despised by all, but s/he can start with a fresh character, apply the lessons learned and try again, without the threat of losing RL status, friends, or risking physical or other RL reprimands. A 40 year old female player noted, "It's a good lab for trying out different strategies for meeting people, requesting assistance, forming/leading teams, etc., where a failure, at worst, means I'll abandon that mud rather than having RL consequences." Not even does one always have to start over with a completely new character, Graye describes how his character keeps changing and how he incorporates changing sensibilities in his character's personality.

> [I]n many ways, Graye is more complex than a normal character, because he's mostly a reflection of my persona, but without many of the social restrictions applied, scary as that may be. in other ways, he's barely a character, because I haven't bothered to define him. I leave him open to the situation... he changed with my moods, my ideas, and my current frame of mind. in a sense, he's a vessel for what I can't express or don't express IRL. [...] if you have a character that doesn't change.. he gets boring, and you kill him off. S'why I'ave had Graye for 3 years... he always changes, and I always have fun with him.

Players tend to mostly play off of aspects of their characters that they in some way find gratifying. Creating a gratifying experience does not necessarily have to include love, care and mutual acceptance, on the contrary, on Cybersphere IC aggressiveness and violence is quite common. Players complaining about too much player-killing or aggressiveness are frequently reminded that "this is

NOT happy fluffy bunny MOO!!!"[66] If they want snuggly role-play and lots of moo.sex, they are advised to go ElseMOO,[67] because Cybersphere is "realistic, violent... hardcore."

Violence and aggression are quite strictly regulated aspects of everyday life and especially killing is subject to severe punishment IRL. Aggression and player-killing can be seen as part of the game, an option open to the player to achieve certain goals in the game (when the killing is part of a plot or simply to gain equipment from the killed character). On the other hand, since the aggression or player-killing is acted out in the MUD, the player can safely experiment with the boundaries and reactions to aggressive behavior, without having to worry about RL consequences, punishment or hir own moral objections. Tôsama at one point remarked:

> I can see how some behaviors started online could be adopted IRL. If a person finds some things done in VR satisfying... (e.g., aggressive behaviors; abusive language, etc.)... they could be adopted IRL, until such time as they become extinguished/discouraged IRL. There might be some inhibitions, but... it's possible.

I think that the carry-over of aggressive behavior from virtual to everyday reality is not particularly great. The differences between everyday reality and the MUD are quite clear to most players and they are aware of the RL consequences. One 28 year old male player answered, when asked if he'd learned anything from role-playing, "Perhaps only the idea that negotiation is still and always a better first choice than combat." An often heard explanation of aggressive behavior in the MUD is that the player "has to let of some steam," "needs to vent" the aggression pent up during hir real life day. A 30 year old female player said, "I like it when I've worked and I got stressed to go kill some monsters, it does help as a stress reliever :)" This mirrors Fine's conclusion that "[g]amers use catharsis to explain and justify the aggressive parts of their gaming..." (1983: 57).

Apart from a blowvalve for frustration the MUD also functions as a space for other experiments. In the MUD the player can experiment with different personality traits and behaviors and test them in a realistic environment where s/he gets realistic feedback. Amy Bruckman (1992) called the MUD an "identity workshop" and Sherry Turkle, from a psychologist's point of view, also stresses the developmental qualities of MUDs, saying that "[t]he Internet has become a significant social laboratory for experimenting with the constructions and reconstructions of self..." (1995: 180). A 19 year old player remarked, "A character's experiences can cause you to take a different look at your own beliefs, from an outside perspective. Sometimes we get lost in our own perspective and can fail to see it from someone elses. Your character can change that, and allow you to see things differently." There seem to be three basic "modes" through which players analyze/evaluate their experiments. The first is by explicitly trying out different behaviors or highlighting certain aspects of the character. Shadowschild on two occasions commented on the role that her character played for her.

I asked Shadowschild if she wanted her character to be more special, more glamorous than she herself is IRL.

<OOC> Shadowschild says, "I think that perhaps that is not true."
<OOC> You say, "do explain..."
<OOC> Shadowschild says, "I don't want Shad to be more 'glamorous' than irl..."
<OOC> Shadowschild says, "She is.. kinda like my 'other self'. She is a place where I can try out new things... new behaviours and new ideas... but she is totally real, to me.. I try to make her behave in a very realistic fashion..."

Shad is my other self. She does things I could never bring myself to do IRL... she is very bold and audacious and challenging. She is fun. She also personifies my most deeply held values and beliefs. But she is not me. I used to be very very shy. Shad has helped me to try out behaviours in a safe environment before I try them IRL. I am much more outgoing and social than I used to be, thanks to my character.

The second "mode" is for the player to be confronted with certain behavior or character traits of hir character. Usually the player recognizes the behavior or character traits as hir own because of the distancing effect of seeing hir reactions echoed back to hir by the MUD-program, which displays what s/he typed in as an action of hir character. A 32 year old female player comments:

There are times that my characters react a certain way in a situation and I recognize that behaviour as being part of my own, or a way that I would have acted in the past. I often liken my first and primary character to myself circa 10 years ago. I've changed somewhat since then, and now when I see that behaviour in her it makes me want to pick her up by the shoulders and shake some sense into her! But over the two years that I've played her she has grown up much the same as I did. I think sometimes it's good to watch roleplay and recognize traits in one's character that one also finds in oneself, so you can decide if it's something that you want to change. But for the most part, it's my RL experience

> that ends up being applied to my character, and not the other way around.

The third "mode" is, as the above example already says, applying your RL experiences to playing your character, in a sense reliving those experiences and testing the responses you got IRL against those you get in the MUD.

One of the processes by which the player gains insight is the exaggeration of the character's traits or behavior. By exaggerating the aggressiveness, the femininity or the physique of your character it becomes more pronounced, eliciting more pronounced reactions.

> Coleman has argued that games provide a caricature of social life... and it is the processes of constructing these caricatures that are of interest. By simplifying and exaggerating, games tell us about what is "real." (Fine 1983: 7)

This corresponds closely with Turner's discussion of how culturally salient aspects of the physical and the cultural body are amplified in order to divorce them from the everyday framework in which they normally are embedded. The use of extreme behavior or stereotypes in the construction of characters is not necessarily a sign of the player's incompetence at constructing a believable character, it can also be an attempt of the player, consciously intended or not, to experiment with or understand particular stereotypes through the more pronounced reactions s/he will receive. Not just the reactions of others here are important, the way it "feels" to enact certain behavior or character traits is important for the player too.

With feeling what the character would feel like we return to the body. For a moment the text may have had it appear that the experimenting the players do is all a very clean and transparent process, that player and character remain separated, drawing on each other's experiences and knowledge in a distanced way. It is not; if the text had it so appear then that's a result of "unfortunate grammar" (cf. Butler 1990: 272) that separates the subject from hir body and bestows 'things' such as "thoughts" with the same "objecthood" as "apple pie and Fords" (cf. Tyler 1987: 155). Graye remarks,

> sometimes, I get adrenaline rushes. Other times, I'll get physically excited. once in a while, something will make me feel ill, or guilty. RP is never wholly objective. if it is, it's not that interesting. emotion and personal interaction often carries across the net, which is why you can tell a person's mood by the text they write. I generally find it quite easy to tell if a person is laughing IRL, joking, or whether they're being sarcastic, just by their syntax. how they phrase things speaks volumes... often more than how it should. it's like the text, in context with the mental reactions to the situations, produces a false

> `experience....a shadow of an IRL experience, but enough to create the emotions.`

The body can be and *is* affected by the text; the text evokes a body that evokes a text; or maybe more in the line of Tyler's argument (1993), [the] text evokes [a] body [that] evokes [a] text. The game is not about winning, it is not about experience points, it is about experience. Experience that evokes emotion, experience that evokes the possibilities and alternatives of everyday reality in fantasy. "If the player doesn't care about his character then the game is meaningless" (Fine 1983: 185), but if the player is sufficiently engrossed in the game, then the experience is more than just the "shadow of a RL experience." Turkle tells the particularly interesting story of a woman who has lost a leg in a car accident. By creating a character that also has lost a leg and thus also features a prosthesis she learns to deal with her loss IRL. The personal transformation that this woman has experienced is quite pronounced and I think usually players don't feel that their online experiences amount to quite so much. However, change is a gradual process and

> [h]aving literally written our online personae into existence, we are in a position to be more aware of what we project into everyday life. Like the anthropologist returning home from a foreign culture, the voyager in virtuality can return to a real world better equipped to understand its artifices. (Turkle 1995: 263)

The player in a sense undertakes a vision quest; s/he travels through a metaphorical world that conjoins fantasy and reality in the disconnected or exaggerated imagery of hir everyday life in search of a restorative vision that will let her

> [c]onsider why we construct the past and indeed the present in a particular way at a specific point in time and space. [S/he] can then consider representations for the way they shape what can and can't be said or thought, and the relation these representations have to wider social, cultural and governmental processes. (Blackman: 140)

Tyler calls the image of the Other, of the "noble savage" painted in the ethnography, "a therapeutic image" (1987: 204), while Mitchell (1989) shows that the image of the Orient functions as the a constitutive outside, the "otherness" that at once renders "our" reality as real *and* as more advanced and logical, as "more amenable." The shift of perspective that we seek, that we think provides a therapeutic effect, that "allows you to look at your own beliefs, from an outside perspective," does not change reality. It *does* change our construction of reality, to quote Bakhtin once more,

> [m]eaning cannot (and does not wish to) change physical, material, and other phenomena; it itself is stronger than any force, it changes the total contextual meaning of an event and reality without changing its actual (existential) composition one iota; everything remains as it was but it acquires a

completely different contextual meaning (the semantic transformation of existence). (Bakhtin in Schultz 1990: 141)

The reason that we should be questing for a therapeutic image is the well covered paradox at the heart of the "Western" discourse. A paradox, as Whorf (1956) showed, rooted deep in the grammar of "Standard Average European" languages (cf. Hendriks and Schaap 1995; Tyler 1987, Ch. 5 et passim). It is the "originary disjunction between signifier and signified..." (Tyler 1987: 10) that separated the world from the word that recreated the world in our word and cast it up for mental manipulation. Representation is based on this separation of signifier and signified, where one is said to stand for the other, where the word is the world to us, while cleverly hiding the fact that it merely is a word. It is this obscurantist principle that lies at the heart of the separation of "real" and "virtual," of "abject" and "virtuous," of "conscious" and "subconscious," of "fantasy reality" and "reality fantasy." The therapeutic image we seek in high-tech is an archaic medicine for the pain of atonement for that original sin, the appropriation of the world in the word.

The cover illustration (*Cyborg* by Lynn Randolph) of Donna Haraway's book *Simians, Cyborgs, and Women* is very telling in this respect. Imagine one of those Apollo mission photographs taken on the moon. Not that picture with Earth floating in the 'sky,' but one of the lesser publicized pictures where the bottom quarter of the image is a barren, hilly, starkly lit landscape and the three quarters of the image up from the ragged horizon is the deepest black of the universe, with distant stars as pinpricks in the canvas. Central in the picture, towering up in mythical proportions from behind the horizon, as if sitting at a table, is a woman with long, dark hair. Her elbows rest on the horizon, her arms stretch forward into the landscape, and her fingers are resting on the keys of a "keyboard" that spring from the very landscape like neatly arranged, flat-topped high-rises. Behind the woman, in the vast expanse of the

```
Save, redo or abandon (s/r/a):
You write the message on the board.

*** The portal message board ***

PT: 929015003 From: Sig , 10/6/1999 at 07:43

fresh allotment of harddisk space
wriggling my words into crevices
the gigantic magneto resistance heads
manipulated by my typing fingers
thousands of miles from the actual apparatus
-
as if i snake/sneak out over the wires
in the dark night of the black fluorescent
screen
my actions silently/dutifully echoed back to
me
-
spin platters spin!
and my archaic words will rest
in your firm magnetic grip.
```

universe, floats a computer screen, filled with renderings of nebulae, black holes, mathematical formulae and a 3D wire frame of some sort of vortex. Draped on the woman's head and shoulders is a lion's skin. The lion's head rests on top of the woman's head and the lion's front legs and paws, translucent as in an aboriginal painting, showing bone structure and ligaments, stretch down over her shoulder. The woman's chest shows the traces of an integrated circuit, at the center of which, embedded in her chest it seems, there is something that looks like a block of dipswitches or maybe a microprocessor. The image evokes a sense of shamanistic high-tech. The universe of the computer turned inside-out, a vast "inter-" or "other-space", where clean, objective high-tech is intermingled, mangled, MUDdled with myths of origin and arcane knowledge of an other kind. "It is the story of the necessity for loss and alienation and of the necessary longing for the lost and alienated" (Tyler 1987: 3).

The Last Job

> As she lay dying, her life passed before someone else's eyes.
>
> —Alan Sondheim

The chair tilted backwards and he put his feet up on the cluttered desk. He surveyed the disorganized collection of some fifty vidscreens piping footage into his life. The old monitor showing the back-end of his website beeped again, indicating his latest clip had once more been licensed and a handsome fee deposited on his bank account. Still curious how his work spread across the globe he pulled the keyboard on his lap and punched up the details of the latest licensee.

"Wow," he marvelled softly to the screens. "MSNBC really likes me, an international license... I bet good old Harry is getting a pay raise pretty soon now."

He grabbed a remote and raised the volume of the big vidscreen on top of the industrial strength wall rack, just in time to hear the MSNBC puppet wrap up the announcement of his clip with a dramatic, "...and categorically refusing to comment on the gruesome events earlier today."

He gulped down the last of the now cold coffee, winced, and watched his name light up briefly in the lower right-hand corner of the screen. He raised the volume some more, blotting out the hum of the machinery all around him.

The familiar satellite image of the city fills the main screen, random sounds from the street-side mike as a soundtrack. Then the artificial intelligence image analyzer finds interesting movement patterns and it does a vertiginous split-second zoom. The corp-sector appears as a grainy streetplan, little color-coded specks moving down black-and-white High Street. He punches up the image analysis and enhancement tools and works through the familiar commands, shaping and sharpening the image until High Street fills the screen and you can see a darkly clad person being pursued by two uniformed security guards. The fleeing figure slips through the crowds seemingly without effort while the guards have difficulty keeping up. They crash into people and are just too bulky in all that armor to take advantage of the short stretches of open sidewalk, where the fleeing figure shoots forward.

They are coming up to NCI's headquarters, where his friend Harry is glued to a screen somewhere, taking care of corporate business undoubtedly. He quickly logs in on the account that Harry had secretly set up for him and grabs a joystick to control the surveillance-cam outside the loading bays, feeding his machines with a second vidstream. Good, no vans or trucks unloading; that probably means nobody is paying attention to this cam. He tilts the cam down and sweeps it along High Street, waiting for the fugitive to appear in range of the cam. He fiddles with the settings of the satellite feed, but there's little extra he can gain. Then the black clad figure appears on the screen and he quickly centers the image with the joystick and punches up the intelligent tracking tool, giving it control of the camera. He pulls up a second set of the image enhancement tools and works feverishly to get the contour-management locked on the amazingly agile fugitive. When he finally gets it right, he raises the image clarity and pipes a four-time magnification to a second screen.

He gasps. A girl, dressed in black jeans, a black t-shirt and combat boots gracefully races through the crowd. Her short black hair and her small backpack bob up and down. He leans forward, scrutinizing the pixelated image and then grins, "This is good."

The pursuit continues down High Street and the girl is still gaining on the guards. The telephoto lens of the NCI surveillance cam is zoomed in to its maximum now and produces the kind of flat, compressed looking picture that is inherent to high focal lengths. As the girl approaches Blumenkraft the grin slowly fades from his face. She's heading for the Access Tunnel. She wouldn't, would she? She'd never pass the guards and the gates on the other side. How desperate could she be? Desperate enough it seems.

His fingers fly over the keyboard and he pulls up a citygrid with the locations of his hovercams. Cam4 is still tailing the ambulance downtown, but it's closest. He drags the cam's icon towards the Access Tunnel's entrance and watches the cam's feed go berserk as it races through the streets. Cam3 is in repair and Cam1 is in Old City, so they are of no use *now.* Cam2 hovers around in the docks. The girl races into the heavy traffic and dodges her way across Blumenkraft. Amazing... No time thinking! He drags Cam2's icon towards the

Access Tunnel and turns to Cam4's vidfeed. Almost there. The girl disappears into the Access Tunnel when the guards finally reach the intersection. They slow down and cross the street, posting themselves on each side of High Street, machineguns raised.

Cam4 now hovers outside the Access Tunnel, just in time to see the gates closing and the city-side guards running about, taking their positions. The girl's trapped. Just then a matte-black AV-22 Eviscerator drops from the sky. The wickedly formed hull bears no markings whatsoever. It slams to an abrupt halt a mere few feet from the ground. Several bursts from AV-22's onboard cannons virtually disintegrate the guards before they can even turn around. A small rocket launched from the right wing rips the gates apart. Seconds later the girl appears from the smoke filled tunnel and bolts across the intersection. The AV-22 swivels around in a perfect 360 degrees turn, surveying the area and then it jumps up into the sky, disappearing into the late afternoon sun.

"Jeez..." he mutters, followed by a hearty "Fuck!" as the girl sprints down Fuji Boulevard, disappearing into the crowd on the sidewalk. He grabs the joystick and sends Cam4 after the girl, the cam's image stabilizer only partly able to correct his twitchy steering. When the running girl reappears on his screen he sighs with relief. He sets Cam4 to autotracking and glances at Cam2's vidfeed. It has arrived at the Access Tunnel's entrance and the cam's artificial intelligence routines have it covering the damage. The cam dutifully films the wisps of smoke, the demolished gate and the remaining body parts. A small crowd is already forming at the entrance, people kicking and tugging at blackened pieces of equipment. Sirens sound and an Emergency Team arrives from the south.

Before the Emergency Team can debark their bulky AV-4's, an armored security vehicle wrestles itself through the remains of the Tunnel entrance. It plows through the debris and sends the crowd scuttling out of its path. Security grunts on foot follow closely in the vehicle's wake. He tags the security vehicle for Cam2 to follow and then splits the satellite feed to separately center on the girl and the Access Tunnel's entrance. Despite the cam's distance, he quickly drags Cam3's icon towards the Access Tunnel, knowing it might arrive too late for any action. Action sells, the aftermath is for losers.

Cam4 is following the running girl. She has crossed Fuji and is sprinting along the buildings that make up the money wall. There are less people on the sidewalk here and the cam can do a 360 of her without bumping into anything or anyone. He pulls up the cam's special effects window and selects the 360, ticking the zoom-for-close-up feature. When he clicks the GO button the cam starts its perfectly plotted course around the running girl. He grins tensely at the screen, realizing he's started to mentally call her the Running Girl. As the camera progresses on its curved trajectory the buildings and people on the sidewalk, flattened by the perspective, shift aside like the layered backgrounds of a manga movie. She glances up as the cam enters her peripheral vision, surprise quickly set aside by grim determination. Reaching a three-quarter image the cam starts to zoom in on her face. Her feet pound the sidewalk, her breath harsh but controlled. Her face fills most of the screen, and then the cam is slowly zooming out already. The long light of the low winter sun caresses her face, leaving deep, well-defined shadows.

She's not young, but not very old yet either. Judging from the subtle lines of both grief and joy around her eyes, you'd say she'd have to be in her mid-thirties. She's about five foot five and slender, with firm shoulders. Her thick, black hair is cut short, but it still manages to get in her face now and then. She has high cheekbones and there might well be some Asian blood running through her veins, even as her complexion is definitely Caucasian. Her eyes such a dark green that only in this bright light the green manages to shimmer through.

She wears a ragged tight fitting black Sisters of Mercy T-shirt that has had its sleeves torn out. Under the phosphorous green logo of a stylized sun that runs across her chest it reads, 'Some Girls Wander By Mistake.' A small black backpack rides high on her back, bobbing up and down as she runs. On her left arm, just under her shoulder, sits a little abstract Polynesian tattoo. Its fine lines and little triangles run in a ring around it. On her arms tiny hairs, completely washed white by salt and sun and therefore contrasting with the more bronzed tint of her skin. Her fingers are slender but seem to be a bit shorter than average, giving her hands a bit of a 'petite' look. She wears a pair of comfortable jeans. The jeans probably were black once, judging from the faint grey they are now. On her feet she wears a pair of tough steel toed Dr. Martens.

Then she just disappears. The vidfeed of the cam goes wild as its AI routines have it whizz around searching for their target. Snapping back to reality he whacks the manual override and grabs the joystick. He should have fucking known! Image stabilizers up to maximum and he yanks the cam around. Back to the corner of Midtown and Fuji. There's Club XS. And there's the alley. With this light the cam would never pick up the dark slit in the wall. He slips the cam between the walls and selects the infrared overlay. The alley glows dimly, contours either wickedly sharp or hardly visible because of the infrared. He maneuvers the cam deeper into the alley, scouring the image for the familiar signs of body heat.

Graffiti covers the walls, just as he remembers, and garbage is still heaped against them. Where the walls recede a little the alley forks, a small path through the garbage weaves around an overflowing dumpster. He pauses for a moment, biting his lip. Then he swivels the cam west, peering down that part of the alley. North leads to the warehouse and the possibility of escape. He swivels the cam back and eases it forward. She steps from the shadows, her katana severing the vidfeed.

He stares at the dead pixels.

"Fuck it!" he yells at the screen.

Cam4 hovers above the security vehicle. It is parked in front of the SecuriTech apartment complex way past the alley, if parking is what you'd call it. Two of the vehicle's six wheels have crunched a bench on the sidewalk, skidmarks indicating the path of its abrupt stop. All hell had probably broken loose in the control rooms when the girl disappeared from their screens. He gently floats the cam upwards, up over the roofs and back to the alley's entrance. No need to alert anyone to where he is going by shooting off and making a bee-line for the alley.

Again he steers his cam into the alley, completing the agonizingly slow detour. He shoots the cam forward to the fork and staying high above the ground he takes the northern path. The cam floats forward slowly now. Peering at the image he promises himself to finally invest in microwave radar for his cams when this clip starts to pay off. The dead neon advertising of a tattoo shop manages a feeble flicker every now and again. Carefully dipping down he investigates the body that lies in a pool of blood opposite of the shop's steel door. Slashed open from shoulder to hip it looks like the Running Girl's handiwork. No street thug he quickly concludes, glossing over the expensive gear that spills from the dead guy's ripped micro-weave suit.

He swivels the cam around with a paranoid shiver. Then he sees her. A few metres further down the alley. She sits with her back against the wall, one knee pulled up, almost looking comfortable. Her hands are pressed against her belly, blood is all over. The camera a natural extension of his body, he moves towards her. When he leans over her, she opens her eyes. Her face is white as marble. Her eyebrows accentuating her now heavy, slightly slanted eyelids. Her eyes stare tiredly back at him. Specks of blood are all over her face, her dark hair sticky with it. She blinks slowly at him and her thin lips form a word. Her breath is barely a whisper and he can't make out what she says. She closes her eyes and her chin sinks down on her chest. The garish neon flicker casts an eerie shadow.

The directional mikes of the cam pipe the sound of people approaching into the silence of pure video. He floats up and settles quietly on a ledge. Floodlights blast the shadows from the alley as security guards move forward in single file. They pass the dead guy hardly showing any interest. Finding the girl a suit moves to the front of the line and bends over her with a scanner. The suit produces a pair of surgical scissors from his flak jacket and cuts the t-shirt of the Running Girl away. Her fingers are unlocked and reveal a big shotgun wound just above the waistband of her pants. Her dermal armor is ripped and bend inward. The suit has one of the guards remove her Dr. Martens and then cuts away her pants, revealing a tattoo covering most of her left thigh. He zooms in, exploring the image of a snake crawling up a ritual dagger, reaching for two Japanese characters as if it wants to eat them. Everything is scanned and bagged. Her marble body is turned over, her arms limp, her breasts flattened against the garbage. A huge tattoo of a fierce red tiger covers most of her back, the vibrant colors so very much alive against her cold skin. From upon high he smiles, noticing that her backpack is not there. Whatever she'd tried to say to him, he'll put it out on the Net. The suit consults with one of the guards and has her bagged. The suit then leaves the way he came, very efficiently. The guards carry the black rubber bag after him.

Alone, back in his room, he put the clip together. When most of the video worked, he pulled up the index to his music archive. Relying on instinct he scrolled through the thousands of titles until his hand wavered. He scanned the titles in front of him. Of course... the Subsonic Gamelan Warriors were a perfect score for this. Wicked, traditional Indonesian rhythms, on top of a scorching industrial bass rumble would underscore the speed, the panic, the oppressiveness of the city, the rush of it all...

He put the finished clip up on his server and shot a mail to Harry, giving him first dibs. He leaned back and put his feet up on the desk. She still stared at him from a couple of vidscreens.

Rewriting Illusion

> The realism is an *illusion of realism.*
>
> —Gary Alan Fine, *Shared Fantasy*

In this text I have tried to evoke a sense of an other world. On the one hand the text is riddled with "place-holders," testifying to the eyewitness account of me, as an anthropologist, "having been there" (cf. Geertz 1988), while on the other hand I have tried to undermine the hegemonic discourse of visual acuity and representational excellence where I could. In a sense, this text might be read as a footnote to Stephen Tyler's article *Postmodern Ethnography* (1987, Ch. 6) in that I have, imperfectly, attempted to give (a) voice to some of the concerns that he there addresses. Here I want to draw another analogy, this time between the ethnography and the MUD. In fact, I want to argue that this text is not an ethnography, instead, the MUD *is* the ethnography. In the modernist effort to create a representation of the world that is a perfect depiction of it,

Christopher Pinney, in his hilarious but at the same time deadly serious fictive retirement speech 'written' in the year 2029, foresees the creation of "virtual reality programs."

> Virtual Reality was soon used in anthropology... as a teaching instrument – students were able to "visit" (via a "senso-sheath" [a full body data- glove]) renowned field sites in cyberspace. Data collected in the field, together with satellite-mapped cartographic data formed the basis of Virtual Reality programs that allowed wearers of the "senso-sheath" to walk through Zandeland or Tikopia and converse with informants through speech interface programs, observe ritual – do all the things "real," pre-virtuality anthropologists used to do. (1992: 411-412)

Of course, Pinney's Virtual Reality is one where the environment is fully immersive, where most of the senses (no one ever seems to talk about smell) are stimulated directly, either through a direct neural interface (drawing on Gibson) or some sort of data-gloves (drawing on Rheingold (1991)). One of the problems with these "virtual reality programs" is that the representation is so perfect that it is as real as reality, and hence it offers no analysis or comment, or rather, because its perceptual appearance is so well suited to our Western sensibilities the fact that this recreation is founded in the linguistic, cultural, perceptual and political conventions of that Western discourse is so well hidden that hardly anyone will notice the difference. A slight, ontological difference remains. The "informants" are cleverly programmed artificial intelligences, or "bots" in net.speak. Unless we presuppose – and frankly, although 2029 seems a bit premature to me now, why should we not? – the ability to recreate fully aware consciousnesses in hardware (other than carbon-based "meat") these bots would not be able to "[reach out] to others by portending, pretending, extending, and intending" (Tyler 1987: 18) in a true idiolectical innovation of the discourse. A virtual reality program is thus the epitome of representation, taking the concept of representation so far that the representation is just as good as what it represents, starting the whole process of perception-analysis-representation anew, and like the snake eating its own tail it is thus destined to eventually disappear in the black hole of its own devouring (cf. Hendriks and Schaap 1995).

In his book *The Unspeakable: Discourse, Dialogue, and Rhetoric in the Postmodern World,* Stephen Tyler deconstructs the discourse of modernism. Representation is the key trope of modernism and "[n]othing so well marks the modern urge as this utopian dream of transparent language, of language so perfectly fitted to the world that no difference could insinuate itself between words and things" (Tyler 1987: 7). Tyler, after Bacon (ibid.: 5), calls the modernist mode of writing, "Plain Style." Apart from the strive to perfect language so that it would veritably capture and mirror the world,

> [p]lain style, above all else, seeks to erode the presence of the speaker by eliminating all marks of individuality that speak of the speaker's difference from the text. Speaker intrusions, from personal pronouns to parentheses, must be rigorously controlled. The text should be the unspoken voice of a universal reader immanent in the text at the same time as it transcends it. Plain style presupposes a transcendental ego who is not so much the author of the text as the creator of it. This is how plain style seeks to obliterate the speaker's voice without at the same time undermining the author-ity of the text (ibid.: 7)

The text, authoritative but not authorial, after all should fit the discourse that dictates that subjective observation can be turned into objective, shared knowledge by the ever increasing acuity of the researcher's vision – through the "looking glass" (of) science, the microscope, the telescope and the camera – and the ever more perfected mode of description. Slowly the truth is supposed to be uncovered in a movement from "I see" to "we agree."

> The first person plural, that mark of royalty, of rule, the "we" that justifies and objectifies the subjectivity of the [ay] as the authority of the unauthored is the sign of the modern era's obsession with the method of consensus. Science and democracy are founded in it, as are the corporation, bureaucracy, and all forms of totalitarianism. It is the objective means of the fictions that speak with the authority of the realities they have made, saying "because it is, you must." (ibid.: 3-4)

In the ethnography however, Tyler finds the possibility of a genre, not really a mode of writing, but rather a mode of telling or conveying that doesn't necessarily speak in an authoritative voice and does not pretend to espouse a transcendental truth (although it can do those things as well as any text), rather

> [i]t transcends instead by *evoking* what cannot be known discursively or performed perfectly, though all know it as if discursively and perform it as if perfectly. Evocation is neither presentation nor representation. It presents no objects and represents none, yet it makes available through absence what can be conceived but not presented. It is thus beyond truth and immune to the judgement of performance. It overcomes the separation of the sensible and the conceivable, of form and content, of self and other, of language and the world. (ibid.: 199-200)

Evocation thus is the key concept for the postmodern ethnography and it is one of the reasons for those novelistic and poetic interjections or counterpoints you have been reading. The form that this text has taken is both an experiment and a necessity. Experimental maybe not so much in the different texts' individual expressions, as in their conjunction, and if not experimental for you, it has been for me. Necessary because I felt I could not possibly express, convey, evoke what I needed to within the bounds of the scientific discourse. Another factor is that the scientific discourse, and especially ethnography's stabs at objectivity, the rhetorical ploys to convince the reader of "scientific soundness" and "having been there," can very well conjure up the idea of reality, of a real village with real inhabitants in a real country (which you can find on a real map in a real atlas), but it has a serious deficiency in the department of conjuring up the idea of an imaginary reality as if it were real. Actually, scientific discourse is one big rhetorical ploy to call up an imaginary reality as if it were real, but it must conceal that fact at all costs because its very legitimization is founded on it. Discussing an imaginary reality that subverts the notions of what is real is therefore rather difficult in a discourse that rigorously attempts to obscure and expel that very notion from its discourse.

What I will do then, to return to the analogy between the MUD and the ethnography, is present Tyler's initial description of the postmodern ethnography and then discuss the different elements therein, showing why the MUD *is* a postmodern ethnography and why this text cannot be a postmodern ethnography. The description of the so far hypothetical "postmodern ethnography" that Tyler gives, detailing what it would be like as opposed to the "plain style" writing of science, in order to subvert the totalitarian regime of the scientific discourse, reads as follows:

> A postmodern ethnography is a cooperatively evolved text consisting of fragments of discourse intended to evoke in the minds of both reader and writer an emergent fantasy of a possible world of common sense reality, and thus to provoke an aesthetic integration that will have a therapeutic effect. It is in a word, poetry – not in its textual form, but in its return to the original context and function of poetry which, by means of its performative break with everyday speech, evoked memories of the *ethos* of the community and thereby provoked hearers to act ethically... Postmodern ethnography attempts to recreate textually this spiral of poetic and ritual performance. Like them, it defamiliarizes common-sense reality in a bracketed context of performance, evokes a fantasy whole abducted from fragments, and then returns participants to the world of common sense – transformed, renewed, and sacralized. It has the allegorical import, though not the narrative form, of a vision quest or religious parable. (Tyler 1987: 202)

To make the mental leap from considering the historical, agreed upon idea of the ethnography as an authoritative text produced by the author/researcher to the MUD as an postmodern ethnography, I think it is of crucial importance to let go of the idea of a possibility of closure, of *telos,* of an ultimate truth. The postmodern ethnography is never "whole", it is always just a fragment, itself too consisting of fragments. The text may know an end, but reality or the MUD do not, except in catastrophe; they exist in the never-ending here and now, always already here and still there a second later. The character may die, a plot-line may be resolved, but reality, even fantasy reality marches on towards new developments, new plots, new characters, new dialogues (cf. Hendriks and Schaap 1995).

> Because postmodern ethnography privileges "discourse" over "text", it foregrounds dialogue as opposed to monologue, and emphasizes the cooperative and collaborative nature of the ethnographic situation in contrast to the ideology of the transcendental observer. In fact, it rejects the ideology of "observer-observed", there being nothing observed and no one who is observer. There is instead the mutual, dialogical production of a discourse, of a story of sorts. We better understand the ethnographic context as one of cooperative story making which, in one of its ideal forms, would result in a polyphonic text, none of whose participants would have the final word in the form of a framing story or encompassing synthesis – a discourse on the discourse. (Tyler 1987: 203)

The MUD *is* that text, it *is* the postmodern ethnography. It is a text, from the source-code of the MOO-program and the objects that make up the world to the most intimate details of the characters and their every dialogue.

The MUD is a text that has evolved cooperatively from the different people who wrote the program-lines of the source-code and the initial room-descriptions to the discussion between two characters thoroughly immersed in their virtual reality that takes place in real-time. A text also that is fragmented to the extreme. The text resulting from a database dump would show the total and utter dispersion of fragments of text, a carnival of deconstruction magically woven together by the MOO-program into the semblance of a world. A lot of the text in the database dump is even hardly readable at all, it consists of code that will be reconstituted on the fly by the MOO, as for instance in the case of the pronoun-substitutes, which yield different results depending on who "calls upon them". Most dialogues are fragmented too, interspersed with pages from other players, OOC banter, game related messages, and often too those things that happen outside the frame of the telnet client, like writing e-mail or HTML, a phone call, a boss or girl/boyfriend walking in, etc. In that sense, the examples presented throughout this text have been "cleaned up" a bit too much, with the exception maybe of Shadowschild's "object lesson" about having to react in a socially expected manner.

While the MUD is textual, discourse at all times prevails over text. The surest indicators are the abundance of typos, mangled grammar and spelling, and trailing periods indicating pauses or thoughts. Communication, getting the message across, dialogue is central. You don't have hours to compose a paragraph until it's perfect, your response is needed here and now, and whatever you come up with will have to do. There is quite a bit of leeway when dealing with incongruencies and inconsistencies, but there is little understanding for "monologues". It's simply no fun, and thus not engrossing, to be told how your character reacts by another player. Getting caught in "monological" moo.sex would seem the worst example of this and the situation has had me close to giving up and logging out more than once. When one of the two (or more *grin*) participants virtually ignores your emotes and simply acts out hir own fantasy, "directing" what happens and dictating even how the other participant(s) feel, then every possibility for identification and thus engrossment is taken away. The text is ad hoc and only the shared effort will vividly call up the fantasy reality as if it were real.

The MUD is a polyphonic text if there ever was one and I think it is safe to say that none of the players, or even the bits, will ever have the final word. The discussions that rage on the BBS, and especially in Meta, testify to that. Every player is entitled to voice hir ideas, gripes, remarks in public and few don't keep their end up in Meta. Not only will the players never stop quibbling about the arcane inner functioning of the game (and especially the code that organizes the combat) and what "role-playing" actually means, but also is there hardly a moment of the day when there is nobody role-playing. I have found myself logged in to Cybersphere at rather odd hours as the only player and still I "emoted out" my character. I emoted sitting all alone at the bar, ordering a drink now and again from the bot-bartender, going through my stuff and thinking things over. And I believe I'm not alone in doing this. In a Meta discussion one of the players said,

```
Smiley said something quite some time ago about the best
role playing he ever does is when he's alone. yeah. I'd have
to agree with him on that.
```

I think that when players create an "internal" dialogue, acting out their characters, even in absence of other characters, this gives a good indication of the pervasiveness of dialogue on the MUD. It testifies to the engrossing character of the virtual world that has been created, so much so that even if you're all by yourself the reality of the game is so compelling that you still act out your character; the fantasy reality has become so incorporated that it no longer becomes meaningless when it's not shared at a particular moment.

Dialogue, role-play is the heart of the game. It is "a story of sorts", one in which every participant is both a reader and a writer and every reader/writer is part of the evocative project that is the shared fantasy reality.

> As the utopians knew, ethnography can perform a therapeutic purpose in evoking a participatory reality, but they were wrong in thinking that reality could be explicitly projected in text. It is this echo, then, of participatory reality that the postmodern ethnography seeks to evoke by means of a participatory text in which no one has the exclusive right of synoptic transcendence. Because it is participatory and emergent, postmodern ethnography

> cannot have predetermined form, for it could happen that participants would decide that textualization itself is inappropriate... (ibid.: 205)

In the MUD textualization remains necessary, but in the mean time the number of possible, co-existent realities explodes. In every role-playing situation the MUD's reality is recreated, called up in a particular form and shape suited to the players' momentary needs. Story-lines multiply and diverge, maybe to never meet again. You and I fall in love and start a relationship, while you get yourself into big trouble with a local crime-lord. In the mean time the neighbors plan a coup and the assassination of the mayor. On channel 23 there is an interview with Napoleon Champaign, who painted a very humane portrait of a boostergang in his ethnography but who ended up having his arms cut off for profit by that very same boostergang. Darn, those are nifty prosthetics.

There is no single point of view in the MUD, and because the world and the dialogue are as fragmented as they are, every player will form hir own understanding of that world, necessarily "abducted from the fragments."

> Because its meaning is not in it but in an understanding, of which it is only a consumed fragment, it is no longer cursed with the task of representation. The key word in understanding this difference is "evoke," for if a discourse can be said to "evoke," then it need not represent what it evokes, though it may be a means to a representation. Since evocation is nonrepresentational, it is not to be understood as a sign function, for it is not a "symbol of", nor does it "symbolize" what it evokes. The postmodern text has moved beyond the representational function of signs and has cast off the encumbrances of the substitution of appearances, those "absences" and "differences" of the grammatologist. (ibid.: 206)

This text then is not a postmodern ethnography. Experimental as it may be, I as the author have eliminated all dialogue, because dialogue rendered as text is no longer dialogue, but text masquerading as a dialogue (cf. Tyler 1987: 66). Nor has this text been a cooperative effort, let alone that my "informants" have had any say in the way I have constructed it. The text is thus not polyphone and certainly is authorial, but not too authoritarian I hope. And whether it's evocative in the sense that Tyler hints at, I doubt it, although it may certainly be 'just' evocative. Even though it may evoke a sense of an other world, it is not a shared world. And eventually, this text is still rather rooted in the scientific discourse, maybe less focused directly on representation, but still, secretly, hoping for a truth to be found. The MUD however is truly founded on dialogue, fragmented and fragmenting discourse, and a polyphonic sharing of a fantasy reality, just like everyday reality is and in the following quote postmodern ethnography can be read as MUD.

> Postmodern ethnography captures this mood of the postmodern world, for it too does not move toward abstraction, away from life, but back to experi-

> ence. It aims not to foster the growth of knowledge but to restructure experience, not to understand objective reality, for that is already established by common sense, nor to explain how we understand, for that is impossible, but to reassimilate, to reintegrate the self in society and to restructure the conduct of everyday life. (ibid.: 211-212)

At this point I too must return to everyday reality and the subject I started out with, gender. Gender, so deeply rooted in everyday reality and so thoroughly uprooted in virtual reality and science alike, has been the guiding trope of this text for considering the reality fantasy of Cybersphere and the fantasy reality of the ethnography. The players' constructions and refigurations of gender in role-playing can be read as explorations of possibilities during their time in *limen*, in-between. The bracketing, or rather the problems of truly bracketing everyday reality become especially apparent in the performance of a convincingly gendered character. Role-playing is never wholly objective and the real body tugs at the player, enabling the escape into the cyberspatial realm, while simultaneously preordaining the restorative return of the player to hir everyday reality. The MUD then has become a tool for framing everyday reality. In the extreme case I have found myself in public areas sizing up people, "reading" them as if I were looking for the kind of cues that one finds in character descriptions, while in other, more implicit cases, such as the negotiation of power relations being discursively constructed, I only realized afterwards that I had used knowledge gained through role-playing to understand, to make sense of that particular context. This text attempts to evoke a sense of this metaphorical journey and the possibility of a postmodern ethnography, because it cannot be those things itself.

When returning to everyday reality gender loses its liquid qualities and solidifies, slips back to the moulds that I pried it loose from. I do not aspire to redefine gender, nor the body, for both don't exist as such, except in fantasy. A fantasy nevertheless that is everyday reality, from which I hope to have abducted the reader momentarily. During the reader's absence from hir everyday reality I do hope to have bracketed "gender" for a little while, at least long enough for it to become unsettled, loose from its moorings and set adrift, so that the reader may have been able to imagine other possibilities.

I may not have been able to make my idiolectical innovations stick (cf. Tyler 1987: 18), but maybe the reader now *grins* to hirself when an IC remark sneakily crosses over into RL from the realm of the MUD. By engrossing the reader I may have temporarily enchanted hir enough to at least consider other possibilities and this then, upon return, should be enough to be a bit more aware of the everyday political consequences of such discursive conventions as gender. One of the things that the reader may better understand, is that through their everyday performances people re/create themselves in hierarchies of power. These hierarchies are wholly fictitious, but because "they are, you must." In gender studies and feminist writing the "part" of the woman has been rewritten quite rigorously in the past decades, but because this writing was and is based on a re-routing of power and hierarchy it will have been writing the man's part as well. In a paradoxical, self-defeating twist, gender studies and feminist writing have been kept busy installing the man's part as "higher" and often "repressive," "paternal" or "authoritative," all in order to wrestle out "from under." I believe however, that we should not forget that the hierarchical and social positions we keep writing into existence also rigorously define the man's role. And because this position is being constructed as "higher" and "better", it is being made particularly difficult for those of us who are "written" into that position to not feel at ease with it. It's easy to understand that you want to improve an "inferior" position, but why would someone not be happy "being in control", "being on top of things?" Frankly, because that role is just as restricting, just as constrictive as "not being in control" and "not being on top of things." And if there is one thing that I hope the whole ploy of role-playing has made clear, it is that a stereotypical role does not fit anyone. People who play stereotypical roles somehow are not real. They have incorporated those fictions to the point where they become unreal.

In the end, winking with my forked eye to the players of Cybersphere, I hope I have not offended anyone (well, not too much at any rate) and that they can laugh about the whole deal (cf. Tyler 1987: 66). I also hope that they don't think I have unfairly appropriated/co-opted their/our fantasies. While this text may not be entirely proper to the dictate of dialogue, it may well function as a start for new dialogues and the greatest honor would be if this text somehow becomes embedded in the local history of that violent, but singularly breathtaking city of New Carthage.

Disconnected

She sat there, her back against the wall, the warm life slowly seeping away through her fingers. The fluorescent green of her world lay soothingly in a sea of black. Still, the angry words bit my eyes. The world spun before her eyes and went black, a low humming sound filling her ears...

Slowly, ever so slowly, the thick warmth of her blood allowed me to let go. And I remembered her. The way I always will. The way she sang for me,

> All my words are secondhand and
> Useless in the face of this
> Rationale and rhyme and reason
> Pale beside a single kiss[68]

Notes

1 The acronym MUD stands for 'Multi User Dungeon' and often functions as a generic moniker for different kinds of text-based virtual environments.
2 August 3, 2001 the MUD Connector, located at http://www.mudconnector.com, listed 1808 different MUDS. The MUD Connector offers a fairly extensive list of current MUDS, but since not all MUDS in existence are listed there, I think that one could safely add some 5 to 10 percent to the number mentioned on their pages in order get an estimate on the total number of current MUDS.
3 I first encountered the use of "hir" as a pronoun in Sullivan and Bornstein's intriguing and rich 1996 novel about gender, sexuality and online communication, entitled *Nearly Roadkill.*
4 I have however taken the liberty of giving Doc Benway a couple of lines, whereas in the game Doc Benway is a simple non-player character, a bot sitting in a room called the Operating Theatre where the character can get "advantages" by making a selection on a computer terminal set in one of the walls. At some point cyberdocs were introduced as player-characters and players could then install all kinds of advantages for other players.
5 A note for those mudders going "uhmpf, not _that_ article again," please bear with me for a little while.
6 Danet (1996) lists all 11 available genders of MediaMOO in figure 10 of her article. Some authors mention that it seems plausible that the spivak gender has been derived from the name of postcolonial theorist Gayatri Chakravorty Spivak. The LambdaMOO helpfiles however state: "The spivak pronouns were developed by mathematician Michael Spivak for use in his books. They are the most simplistic of the gender neutral pronouns (others being 'neuter' and 'splat') and can be easily integrated into writing. They should be used in a generic setting where the gender of the person referred to is unknown, such as 'the reader'. They can also be used to describe a specific individual who has chosen not to identify emself with the traditional masculine (male) or feminine (female) gender."
7 Curtis took over the development of the MOO code from Stephen White (aka ghond) and extended it to the first widely used version that is called LambdaMOO (thanks for the information ShadowDragon). LambdaMOO is still around and in terms of total population it is one of the biggest MUDS currently in existence. The MOO program-code has since been used to support numerous other MUDS.

8 These days that network is usually the Internet, itself an endless number of *interconnected* smaller nets. Before the large-scale availability of the Internet MUDS were also played on local systems that one had to 'physically' dial into.
9 The early history of MUDS is more exhaustively described in Bartle (1990) and Reid (1994). While mudding really started attracting a large following once it was set loose on the (then primarily American) interconnected university networks (the Internet) in the mid to late 80s, it is interesting to note that the first developments of MUDS as we know them now lie in Great Britain, where Roy Trubshaw and Richard Bartle developed the first MUD in 1978-1979, now often referred to as MUD1.
10 This of course is only true in the ideal sense of the word. Fine goes to great length to explain how referees and players influence and exert control over each other in order to shape the fantasy according to their own ideas and wishes into a *shared* fantasy world.
11 Tiny-plots are so called after TinyMUD, one of the first MUDS that did not primarily focus on *gaming* (on completing quests and gathering experience points and gold), but on social interaction. On TinyMUD several mechanisms were first implemented to further social role-playing (cf. Young (1994); Bruckman (1993)).
12 In fact, in the MUD there often are several referees running tiny-plots concurrently and/or interlockingly.
13 William Gibson introduced the term "cyberspace" in his 1984 novel *Neuromancer.* In Gibson's idiom there is quite an overlap between the terms "cyberspace" and "matrix". The concept of cyberspace is usually explained as a "consensual hallucination", which Gibson uses in the following line, "He'd operated on an almost permanent adrenaline high, a byproduct of youth and proficiency, jacked into a custom cyberspace deck that projected his disembodied consciousness into the consensual hallucination that was the matrix" (Gibson 1984). Reflecting on the term cyberspace, Gibson later writes, "Assembled word *cyberspace* from small and readily available components of language. Neologic spasm: the primal act of pop poetics. Preceded any concept whatever. Slick and hollow – awaiting received meaning. All I did: folded words as taught. Now other words accrete in the interstices. [...] I work the angle of transit. Vectors of neon plaza, licensed consumers, acts primal and undreamed of... The architecture of virtual reality imagined as an accretion of dreams: tattoo parlors, shooting galleries, pinball arcades, dimly lit stalls stacked with damp-stained years of men's magazines, chili joints, premises of unlicensed denturists, of fireworks and cut bait... These are dreams of commerce. Above them rise intricate barrios, zones of more private fantasy" (Gibson 1991: 27-28).
14 The message for the @ic command printed out to the player reads as follows: "`You go in-character. Your actions now reflect your character and not necessarily yourself.`" Other players in the same room will see a message in which "`Eveline reminds you that she goes in-character. Her actions now reflect her character and not necessarily herself.`"

15 In Cybersphere some characters don't live more than a few hours, but the average life span of a seriously played character is somewhere between three months and a year. There are some characters that last for over three years.
16 To date the cumulative size of the plain text log files has grown to some 80 megabytes.
17 I will use the term "sex" here as the "natural" outcome of Biology's findings; note that Kessler and McKenna state, "We will use gender, rather than sex, even when referring to those aspects of being a woman (girl) or man (boy) that have traditionally been viewed as biological. This will serve to emphasize our position that the element of social construction is primary in all aspects of being female or male, particularly when the term we use seems awkward (e.g., gender chromosomes)" (1978: 7).
18 In this situation only one X chromosome is present, half of the 23rd chromosome pair, the "sex" chromosomes (cf. Kessler and McKenna 1978: 47) is missing.
19 Cf. Spaink (1998: 25), Beeman (1996).
20 And Kessler and McKenna remind us that this includes the "sex" dichotomy.
21 None of the players who responded to the questionnaire stated a "non-western" country as hir place of residence; 71% reported to be living in the USA, 18% in Europe, 4% in Australia, 4% in Canada, and 3% failed to state a place of residence.
22 If you stick to the female/male gender dichotomy there are only 4 permutations for a player and hir character: f-f, m-m, f-m, m-f. As noted before, with the expanded options for choosing a gender for one's character in MUDs this number rises. One could, however, also imagine a situation in which there are more options for the player hirself to choose from besides female or male.
23 "Getting offed" means getting killed.
24 The term MOO here refers explicitly to the implementation of the LambdaMOO program. While descriptions are a universal part of every MUD, the technical details of this (MOO) implementation determine several influential characteristics of *this* virtual world.
25 To be fair, at least the description is more evocative than, for example, "Your average citizen," or "A sturdy, young fellow."
26 If, for instance, you walk into a bar and there are only one or two other characters, it is quite common for all the characters to "look" at each other. If, on the other hand, you walk into a crowded bar where some eight or more characters are present, looking at every character's description would take up so much time that it seriously hampers your ability to react to the ongoing role-playing. In crowded situations I thus only "looked" at characters whom I hadn't seen before or whom I ended up interacting with directly. Because of time differences between the different parts of the world and a dose of chance, I have interacted quite extensively with some characters, while other characters that nevertheless were around for several months I may have passed only a couple of times in the street.

27 These two characters were technically gender neutral, i.e. their @gender was set to neuter, but their descriptions featured male pronouns. Also interesting to see, is that the distribution of female/male *characters* corresponds closely to the female/male distribution of *players*.

28 BBS: Bulletin Board System. A simple in-game message board that allows players to read and post messages under various headings such as "News," "Chat" and "Sex" which are IC and "Meta" which is OOC.

29 This is even more common in social MUDS and Talkers where one can find descriptions of "a joyful fellow, who likes to dance and play ping-pong." Characteristics like that usually aren't visible when you meet someone in the street. Of course, since Cybersphere is a role-playing MOO, this sort of OOC-like description is less common because the players are describing a character and not a persona.

30 The "cyberpunk" genre knows a lot of influences and a good source of references is Larry McCaffery's *Storming the Reality Studio: A Casebook of Cyberpunk and Postmodern Fiction.* Most common references are to William Gibson's defining cyberpunk trilogy, which started in 1984 with *Neuromancer,* Bruce Sterling's novels, and Ridley Scott's 1983 movie *Blade Runner,* and more recently the Wachowski brothers' 1999 movie *The Matrix.*

31 Lillith uses "@desc" here to indicate the general part of her description. In order to set the general part of the description one has to issue the command <`@desc me is A young, well dressed man...`>. The "naked" descriptions are set separately, e.g. <`@naked_arms me is Long and slender...`>, while the descriptions of the clothes are set on the items of clothing.

32 The asterisks are often invoked to indicate an "emotion," *happily*, or even a pose, *nods and brushes some hair from his forehead*. This convention (some people use different symbols, such as -dashes- or <brackets>) lets players quickly qualify a particular statement. These interjections function much like the well known :-) smiley-faces, but offer a bit more freedom of expression.

33 When I asked Lillith what the particular strengths of each gender were, she answered: "`I feel that the strength of a woman is the ways in which her body speaks to her mind.. with men, the opposite is their strength.`" I asked if these strengths were expressed differently in the descriptions and she answered: "`Sometimes. If the person has paid particular attention to what sort of 'male' or 'female' their character is, their description will reflect that, basically, I just complain a lot about very short, sparse, weak @desc's, regardless of their emphasis.`"

34 Some speak of *Actual* or *Physical* Reality, while others stick to Gibson's *cyberspace* versus *meatspace.*

35 A wizard is a 'player' who has special privileges and "powers" that allow hir to program new additions to the MOO program and perform other maintenance duties. Wizards (or "gods," "admin" or "bits") take care of the nuts and bolts operation of the MOO, while often also performing social duties such as organizing plots and settling player disputes. They perform the online equivalent of

the referee's (or DM's or GM's) role, with the obvious difference that wizards do not referee on individual role-playing situations. "George Eliot" is this player's emanation as a wizard, while Lusiphur is her emanation as a character.

36 Shadowschild and I met in a public, but rather quiet bar, *The Last Exit,* specifically to do an interview and we spoke for over an hour before anyone else entered there. When Shadowschild first entered the bar we both perfunctory acted out the meeting of our characters ICly, but Shadowschild immediately stated "I'm OOC here." She however did not use the @ooc command, which displays a "Shadowschild-goes-OOC" message to all present and sets a flag for the character indicating that s/he is OOC. During the interview we both *did* use the OOC command (which is different from the @ooc command) which prepends to each utterance, indicating that the character, or rather the player spoke OOCly. However, when Shadowschild wanted to illustrate how her character would act, she emoted the actions ICly and not OOCly. This partly has to do with the fact that she uses several so-called "socials": commands that yield a preprogrammed line of text. (Were I to type the command <smile> everybody present would see "Eveline smiles happily"; <smile shadowschild> would show to Shadowschild "Eveline smiles at you" while everybody else would see "Eveline smiles at Shadowschild." The same goes for some 60 such commands as <grin>, <sigh>, <snuggle> and <point>.) "Social" commands don't respond to the @ooc command and always output their preprogrammed text ICly. An other reason, I suspect, is that by emoting ICly Shadowschild wanted to teach an "object" lesson, whereby the IC emoting is seen as a really real enactment of/by the character, while emoting OOCly is can be seen as "speaking of that enactment."

37 Note that I deliberately reacted OOCly to Shadowschild's IC emotes. I did this both to indicate that it was me, the player, reacting and not Eveline and to show that even though Shadowschild emoted ICly, I took those emotes to be OOC expressions. Earlier in the conversation I had already underscored me being OOC by "perpetrating" this gender incongruous emote: "`<OOC> Eveline slaps his forehead.`"

38 I asked why he had played the character for as long (several months, possibly as long as six) as he did. Dave answered, "`yeah, I mean, it felt like I had put so much effort into her, plus I had all this cool gear, it wuz kinda hard to just dump her, by far the biggest RP challenge I've had.`" When I asked whether he had learned anything from the experience, he said: "`sadly enough not really, I basically played off of what I could think of, although now that I think about it, I actually did learn a bit more about the way... women do things, talking and acting, etc.`"

39 Cyric uses "directed speech", which lets him speak directly to Shadowschild. Players use directed speech primarily when saying something to one particular person in a crowded room, indicating to all present to whom exactly they are speaking. Sometimes it is also used to indicate that they are particularly focusing on the conversation with *you.*

40 Eveline gazes out over the crowd, but because I use the "pose" command instead of the "emote" command, the MOO program renders my action in the second person singular to me, while the others in the room actually see that "Eveline gazes out over the crowd." The pose command requires the player to enter the action in the first person singular, heightening the sense of involvement, while the emote command requires input in the third person singular. Thus, using the pose command, the MOO program, imitating a referee, tells me (the player) what I (the character) am doing. From the helpfiles:

```
Pose is more powerful (and prettier) than emote because it conjugates your
message for every interested party in the room. Enter your pose as if you
were typing in a first-person voice.

-- Pose recognises the following:
Names -- Exact matches on the aliases of gendered objects in the room.
Pronouns -- Pronouns will match for the last player mentioned.

Additional verbs you wish conjugated to your gender should be prefixed with
a period.

-- For example:
Typed----> .kick chuck, bruising him on his shin as I .laugh madly.
You see    | You kick chuck, bruising him on his shin as you laugh madly.
Chuck sees| Quinn kicks you, bruising you on your shin as he laughs madly.
Others see| Quinn kicks Chuck, bruising him on his shin as he laughs madly.
```

It's also interesting to note here, how one can set the atmosphere by, for instance, referring to a crowd in one's role-playing. There are no other characters present but Eveline, Shadowschild and Cyric, but the bar is understood to be a busy hang-out for deckers (matrix cowboys, netrunners) and by mentioning that crowd explicitly I (the player) create a part of the shared atmosphere for our three characters.

41 Eveline "looks" at Cyric because Shadowschild mentions his shirt and thus "sees" what Cyric looks like.

42 Shadowschild sends me a *page*, which the MOO sets apart from the other text by prepending "`[-] *Shadowschild*`" to her message. Since a page is private, Cyric does not see this message and because pages are considered an IC form of communication on Cybersphere, Shadowschild has typed out "OOC" preceding her message to indicate that it is indeed an OOC message.

43 I send Shadowschild a page back.

44 While the text here appears monolithically, *as a text,* in one piece as if written down fluently, I must underscore that this is just appearance, a transformation of the moment into a "quote" caused by the fact that it has been embedded in another (con)text. Individual utterances appear on the screen several seconds or sometimes even minutes apart. This is due to the fact that each player has to consider what hir character will do or how s/he should react and subsequently

must type out the commands and text representing that course of action. As you can see there is quite a period of time between Cyric saying "Oh, baby.. you do that soo well" and him adding "quite a bit actually.." There is at least enough time for Shadowschild and me to exchange several pages and Eveline to sit down at the bar.

45 See Fine (1983) Chapter 6. Fine uses Goffman's (1974) ideas on frame analysis, "...how human beings reside in finite worlds of meaning, and that individuals are skilled in juggling these worlds" (Fine 1983: 181), to explain how players manage different sets of knowledge and logic to maneuver between fantasy and everyday realities. I will have to leave the discussion of Fine's use of frame analysis applied to online RPGS for another time. It is however important to note what Fine says about engrossment in the light of frame analysis: "Although perhaps contrary to common sense, people easily slip into and out of engrossment. Frames succeed each other with remarkable rapidity; in conversations, people slip and slide among frames. Engrossment, then, need not imply a permanent orientation toward experience" (1983: 183).

46 In pen-and-paper RPGS one usually speaks *for* one's character, telling the referee (and the other players) that, for instance, "My character walks over to the couch and sits down." The referee evaluates this statement and only after s/he gives hir approval does the character *really* walk over to the couch and sits down. In online RPGS there is no referee who watches over the individual actions of players, judging whether they behave appropriately to the theme and *telos* of the game. The responsibility for maintaining the fantasy reality therefore rests to a much greater degree on the shoulders of the individual players and I as a player must decide myself if walking over to the couch and sitting down is a plausible course of action, because the moment I <emote walks over to the couch and sits down.> my character *really* walks over to the couch and sits down.

47 I have edited this RP situation slightly for readability. Every item of clothing has a set of messages that are displayed when taking it off or putting it on. We each took off half a dozen or so items, so I left these two as examples of what these messages look like. I have also edited out several pages from other characters (to which Eveline didn't respond anyway) and a MOO wide message from a wizard.

48 Katana, a traditional, slightly curved, single edged Japanese sword. The katana is said to represent the samurai's soul. A lot of myth surrounds the katana and it is called the best kind of sword ever made. The steel is said to be folded a thousand times and the cutting edge of the blade is hardened under much higher temperatures than the other side, which is kept cooler by having it covered during the hardening process. Thus the blade has an extremely hard cutting edge, while still being flexible enough not to break in combat.

49 As also becomes apparent, different characters' actions may not always follow each other in a strictly chronological order. Another player's composition of a reaction may take so long, or my inspiration for the next emote may be so great, that I enter it even before the other player can react. Often two emotes will ar-

rive almost simultaneously, player A's second emote preceding player B's reaction to player A's first emote. If the "chronology conflict" isn't too great, usually both players will quietly assume that player B's emote must be read as *preceding* player A's second emote, and player B will rush to compose a reply to player A's second emote. If the chronology conflict is too great, then either player A's second emote or player B's emote must be discarded. Often the solution to this problem is not discussed OOCly, but RP simply continues from the last emote as if the incongruous emote preceding it did not occur at all. Another solution is to proceed from the most logical or most desirable emote which is something that *is* often OOCly discussed. For example:

```
You smile to Chali, "indeed... and you must be Chali..."
You extend your hand to Chali.
Chali extends her hand to you, "Yes. Very glad to meet you."
<OOC> Chali giggles, "Okay. I'll take mine [i.e. my emote] back."
```

In the case above I emote taking Lillith's hand, after which Lillith emotes laying several items on the beach. Since the conflict is not very serious – Eveline could have temporarily let go of Lillith's hand or Lillith may have put down those things using only one hand or Eveline 'actually' took Lillith's hand after she'd put those things down – Lillith simply emotes taking Eveline's hand when she's done.

50 While our characters are in the "room" called *East end of the beach,* there is no "room" called "In the water." Our character-objects, the pieces of MOO-code representing us, remain where they are while we emote running down the beach. Had there been a room called "In the water" we might have typed in the command <go water> and our character-objects would have entered that room, in which case upon entering that room a fixed message saying "You dash down the beach towards the surf..." might have been displayed.

51 The MOO automagically notifies you when someone <looks> at you. For the reader's, ahem, pleasure I have pasted in Eveline's description as Lillith would have seen it.

52 Again, I've cut most of the messages of the clothing being put on.

53 The OOC discussion board meant to discuss matters on the (meta-)level of the players (to which players can post messages for all to read) is called "Meta."

54 Since player-characters *can* be killed, frequently discussions are centered on the question whether a character has been killed (PK'ed, or player-killed) with due role-play. One school of thought says that since killing is part of the game there may have been sufficient role-play preceding the killing (in which the killed character may not have taken part because it was a plot to assassinate hir) to legitimize the on sight shooting of a character, while the other school vehemently argues that *all* player killing must (ideally) be consensual, but at least surrounded (not just preceded) by due role-play involving also the soon-to-be-dead character.

55 Definition of spoofing from Whitlock (n.d.):
Spoofing: intentionally attributing virtual actions to another person's identity,

(sometimes with humorous intent). example...
>Spoof Foobar farts.
Foobar farts.
You say, "Gross!"
Foobar is turning red with embarrassment.
NB: anonymous spoofing is not possible on *Cybersphere*, the name of the player using the spoof command is always appended at the end of the line. The result of "spoof Foobar farts" on *Cybersphere* would read "Foobar farts (by Eveline)".

56 Definition of spam from Whitlock (n.d.), "Spam is a large volume of text that in some way imposes on the viewer."

57 Ogre's comment illustrates that the basic mechanisms thought up by the programmers may be converted, inverted or perverted by players to accommodate radically different behavior than the ideal of social interaction that the programmers had in mind (cf. Whitlock (n.d.), Unsworth (n.d), Bruckman (1996) and Dibbell (1993)). Quite a few articles then detail the problems of players misbehaving and the strategies for keeping "law and order" (cf. Mnookin (n.d.; 1996), Katsh (1996)).

58 Of course, researchers need to justify their work to some extent and tellingly some of Curtis' later papers attempt to do just that; e.g. the title of a 1993 paper co-written with Nichols is "MUDS Grow Up: Social Virtual Reality in the Real World."

59 If we look more closely at the structure of the MOO we see that it is build entirely from objects and that the originating/original object (#0) is the universe, which holds all other objects. Object #1 is the root object, the most generic object of which all the other objects are "children." Object #2 is Arch, the arch-wizard, the god, the owner of the MOO. The only person more powerful than Arch is the person with hir finger on the power-switch of the computer that runs the MOO. Unix and MOOS are "command interpreters" in that the user/player enters commands that are parsed and executed, and the resulting changes in the "environment" are communicated back to the user/player. Unix and MOOS are "user extensible from within" in that both offer the user/player the possibility to extend the functionality *of* the program by writing new routines in a language provided *by* the program.
Kingfox, one of the wizards of Cybersphere, told me the following intriguing story: "Ever see the old TV show the Prisoner? Actually, it's British. From the 60s or 70s I believe. Anyway, the Prisoner has some funny similarities to MOOS, and [Cybersphere]. The main character ends up in the Village, a place he cannot escape. No one is allowed to use names, everyone has a number. He is number 6. The village is run by number 2. The whole time, number six quests to either escape or figure out who is number 1. Last episode, he rips off the mask of number 1, and sees first an alien, then himself, then a gorilla. Now – the similarities. #6 is the generic player. #2 is the archwiz. #1 is the root (primal) object. Ain't that creepy?"

60 Unsworth references this quote as follows: Karl Marx, Economic and Philosophical Manuscripts (1844).
61 The pronouns for the non-conventional genders are of course different from the "regular" male and female pronouns. For the spivak gender for instance they are: e, em, eir, eirs, eirself; example: e reads eir book to eirself. For a full list see Danet (1996), Figure 10. Available Genders on MediaMOO and Lambda MOO.
62 The %N is thus a variable for the player's name, %p is the possessive pronoun (which can be capitalized by using %P) and %r is the reflexive pronoun.
63 Shadowschild illustrates the 'compelling' reasons to conform with an example from her RL, "[p]art of the image, at least for females, is wearing what is socially defined as 'feminine' clothing and accessories. I've found that, in my case, it has often worked that way... Like I said before.. i was a vet assistant... Now I am a copyeditor... but I have found it very difficult to make that change, because I have not been able to afford the expensive clothing and accessories required... and because I refuse to wear a skirt. I have been told that I cannot... CANNOT apply for a job... not because I was not qualified.. not because I was crude, dirty or generally unpleasant to be around... but simply because I would not wear a skirt. I insisted on wearing slacks or pants."
64 I don't think, like Mazur indicates, that this really problematizes the real/virtual dichotomy further, it simply "raises" the level of the "orders of simulacra" by one, making "reality" a first order simulacrum and "virtual reality" a second order one. Rather, I think that it problematizes "reality", in the sense that it becomes inaccessible. In the same fashion that Butler does not question the actual materiality of the body, I do not question the actual materiality of "the reality out there". Reality out there may be a brute fact of life, it is only a meaningful, "legible" fact of life in our everyday construction of it, which is why Baudrillard says it is not real anymore. Maybe it never even existed.
65 The fact that punishment or that other physical violation, rape (cf. Mazur (n.d.); Dibbell (1993)), can be constructed as a "linguistic fact," as the result of the way in which the discourse constructs power relations, I think does not detract from the fact that there is a pointed difference in the "level" of harm done to the body (constructed or not) in a virtual versus a real bodily punishment or rape.
66 A typical rant looks something like this: you want whips, chains, and cute fluffy bunnies?... go to lambdaMOO... -m[ail] me if ya dont have the telnet address...
67 "ElseMOO" is the generic name for any other MOO. It's usage is twofold: either players are told to go there if they don't like it here, or players can say "I'm also playing a character ElseMOO" if they don't want to be specific about which MOO they're playing on.
68 From *Some kind of Stranger* by The Sisters of Mercy.

References

A somewhat regularly updated list of links for the online articles can be found on my homepage, located at: http://www.fragment.nl/resources/

Balsamo, Anne

1996 *Technologies of the Gendered Body. Reading Cyborg Women.* Durham and London: Duke University press, 1997.

Bartle, Richard

1990 *Early MUD History.* Available: http://www.ludd.luth.se/mud/aber/mud-history.html

Baudrillard, Jean

1983 *Simulations.* (Translation from French) New York: Semiotext(e), Inc.

Beeman, William O.

1996 "What are you? Male, Merm, Herm, Ferm or Female?" In: *Baltimore Morning Sun,* March 17, 1996, Edition: F, Section: Perspective Page: 1F. Available: http://songweaver.com/gender/whatru.html (July 27, 2001)

Blackman, Lisa M.

1998 "Culture, Technology and Subjectivity. An 'Ethical' Analysis." In: Wood, John (ed.) *The Virtual Embodied. Presence | Practice | Technology.* London and New York: Routledge, 1998.

Bruckman, Amy S.

1992 *Identity Workshop. Emergent Social and Psychological Phenomena in Text-Based Virtual Reality.* Available: http://www.cc.gatech.edu/fac/Amy.Bruckman/papers/index.html#IW

1993 "Gender Swapping on the Internet." In: Ludlow, Peter (ed.) *High Noon on the Electronic Frontier. Conceptual Issues in Cyberspace.* Cambridge, Massachusetts: The MIT Press, 1996. Available: http://ftp.game.org/pub/mud/text/research/gender-swapping.txt

1996 *"Democracy" in Cyberspace: Lessons from a Failed Political Experiment.* Available: http://anxiety-closet.mit.edu/afs/athena.mit.edu/org/w/womens-studies/OldFiles/www/bruckman.html

Butler, Judith

1990 "Performative Acts and Gender Constitution." In: Sue-Ellen Case (ed.), *Performing Feminisms.* Baltimore: John Hopkins University Press. Pp. 270-283.

1993 *Bodies that matter. On the discursive limits of "sex".* New York and London: Routledge.

Cherny, Lynn

1994 *Gender Differences in Text-Based Virtual Reality.* Available: http://www.fragment.nl/mirror/index.html

Curtis, Pavel

1992 "Mudding: Social Phenomena in Text-Based Virtual Realities." In: Ludlow, Peter (ed.) *High Noon on the Electronic Frontier. Conceptual Issues in Cyberspace.* Cambridge, Massachusetts: The MIT Press, 1996. Available: http://www.eff.org/pub/Privacy/Security/Hacking_cracking_phreaking/Net_culture_and_hacking/MOO_MUD_IRC/curtis_mudding.article

Curtis, Pavel and David A. Nichols

1993 MUDs Grow Up: Social Virtual Reality in the Real World. Available: http://ftp.game.org/pub/mud/text/research/MUDsGrowUp.txt

Danet, Brenda

1996 *Text As Mask: Gender and Identity on the Internet.* Available: http://atar.mscc.huji.ac.il/~msdanet/mask.html

Dibbell, Julian

1993 *A Rape in Cyberspace or How an Evil Clown, a Haitian Trickster Spirit, Two Wizards, and a Cast of Dozens Turned a Database Into a Society.* Available: http://ftp.game.org/pub/mud/text/research/VillageVoice.txt

1998 *My Tiny Life. Crime and Passion in a Virtual World.* New York: Henry Holt and Company.

Fine, Gary Alan

1983 *Shared Fantasy. Role Playing Games as Social Worlds.* Chicago: The University of Chicago Press.

Foucault, Michel

1975 *Discipline, Toezicht en Straf. De Geboorte van de Gevangenis.* (Dutch translation from French) Groningen: Historische Uitgeverij Groningen, 1989.

Geertz, Clifford

1973 "Notes on the Balinese Cockfight." In: Geertz, Clifford *The Interpretation of Cultures.* London: Fontana Press, 1993.

1988 *Works and Lives. The Anthropologist As Author.* Stanford University Press, 1990.

Gibson, William

1984 *Neuromancer.* New York: Ace Books.

1986 *Count Zero.* New York: Ace Books.

1988 *Mona Lisa Overdrive.* New York: Bantam Books.

1991 "Academy Leader." In: Benedikt, Michael (ed.) *Cyberspace: First Steps.* Cambridge, Massachusetts: MIT Press.

Goffman, Erving

1974 *Frame Analysis.* Cambridge: Harvard University Press.

Hendriks, Sander & Frank Schaap
1995 *Met Gespleten Tong of Door het Oog van de Etnografie.* Unpublished paper. Available from author.

Katsh, Ethan
1996 *Out of Context: Dispute Resolution in Cyberspace.* Available: http://anxiety-closet.mit.edu/afs/athena.mit.edu/org/w/womens-studies/OldFiles/www/katsh.html

Kessler, Suzanne J. and Wendy McKenna
1978 *Gender. An Ethnomethodological Approach.* Chicago and London: University of Chicago Press, 1985.

Lakoff, George & Mark Johnson
1980 *Metaphors We Live By.* Chicago: University of Chicago Press.

Little, Kenneth
1991 "On Safari: The Visual Politics of a Tourist Representation." In: Howes, David (ed.) *The Varieties of Sensory Experience. A Sourcebook in the Anthropology of the Senses.* Toronto: University of Toronto Press.

Ludlow, Peter (ed.)
1996 *High Noon on the Electronic Frontier. Conceptual Issues in Cyberspace.* Cambridge, Massachusetts: The MIT Press. Available: http://semlab2.sbs.sunysb.edu/Users/pludlow/highnoon.html

Markham, Annette N.
1998 *Life Online. Researching Real Experience in Virtual Space.* Walnut Creek: Altamira Press.

Mazur, Tomasz
1994 *Working Out the Cyberbody: Sex and Gender Constructions in Text-Based Virtual Space.* Available: http://www.well.com/user/tmazur/research/sexgen.html

McCaffery, Larry (ed.)
1991 *Storming the Reality Studio. A Casebook of Cyberpunk and Postmodern Fiction.* Durham and London: Duke University Press, 1993.

McRae, Shannon
1997 "Flesh Made Word. Sex, Text and the Virtual Body." In: Porter, David (ed.) *Internet Culture.* New York: Routledge.

Mead, Margaret
1935 *Sex and temperament in three primitive societies.* London: Routledge & Kegan Paul, 1977.

Mitchell, Timothy
1989 "The World as Exhibition." In: *Comparative Studies in Society and History, No. 31.* Pp. 217-236.

Mnookin, Jennifer L.
N.D. *Bodies, Rest and Motion: Law and Identity in LambdaMOO.* Available: http://anxiety-closet.mit.edu/afs/athena.mit.edu/org/w/womens-studies/OldFiles/www/mnookin.html

1996 *Virtual(ly) Law: The Emergence of Law in LambdaMOO.* Available: http://www.ascusc.org/jcmc/vol2/issue1/lambda.html

Pinney, Christopher

1992 "Future Travel. Anthropology and Cultural Distance in an Age of Virtual Reality, or, A Past Seen from a Possible Future." In: Taylor, Lucien (ed.), *Visualizing Theory. Selected Essays from V.A.R. 1990-1994.* New York: Routledge, 1994.

Pondsmith, Mike & Colin Fisk & Will Moss & Scott Ruggels & Dave Friedland & Mike Blum

1990 *Cyberpunk 2020. The Roleplaying Game of the Dark Future.* Sourcebook, second edition. Berkeley, CA: R. Talsorian Games Inc.

Quittner, Josh

1994 "Johnny Manhattan Meets the Furry Muckers. Why playing MUDS is becoming the addiction of the '90s." In: *Wired 2.03,* pp. 92-97 & 138. Available online: http://www.wired.com/wired/archive/2.03/muds.html

Reid, Elizabeth M.

1994 *Cultural Formations in Text-Based Virtual Realities.* Available: http://people.we.mediaone.net/elizrs/cult-form.html

Rheingold, Howard

1991 *Virtual Reality.* London: Mandarin Paperbacks, 1992.

Saussure, Ferdinand de

1916 *Course in General Linguistics.* (Translation from French) New York: McGraw-Hill Book Co.

Schultz, Emily A.

1990 *Dialogue at the Margins. Whorf, Bakhtin, and Linguistic Relativity.* Madison, Wisconsin: University of Wisconsin Press.

Spaink, Karin

1998 *M/V, doorhalen wat niet van toepassing is.* Amsterdam: Nijgh en Van Ditmar.

Stone, Allucquère Rosanne (Sandy)

1995 "Sex and Death among the Disembodied. VR, Cyberspace, and the Nature of Academic Discourse." In: Star, Susan Leigh (ed.) *The Cultures of Computing.* Oxford, UK: Blackwell Publishers, 1995.

Sullivan, Caitlin & Kate Bornstein

1996 *Nearly Roadkill. An Infobahn Erotic Adventure.* London and New York: High Risk Books/Serpent's Tail.

Tolkien, J.R.R.

1968 *The Lord of the Rings.* (Originally published in 1954 and 1955 in three volumes) London: HarperCollins Publishers, 1991.

Turkle, Sherry

1995 *Life on the screen. Identity in the Age of the Internet.* London: Phoenix, 1997.

Turner, Victor
1964 "Betwixt and Between. The Liminal Period in 'Rites de Passage'." In: Turner, Victor *The Forest of Symbols. Aspects of Ndembu Ritual.* Ithaca and London: Cornell University Press, 1967.

Tyler, Stephen A.
1987 *The Unspeakable. Discourse, Dialogue, and Rhetoric in the Postmodern World.* Madison, Wisconsin: The University of Wisconsin Press.
1993 *Vile Bodies – A Mental Machination.* (Presented at the 1993 international conference "Body Images, Language and Physical Boundaries" at the University of Amsterdam, The Netherlands) Available: http://people.a2000.nl/fschaap/mirror/index.html

Unsworth, John
N.D. *Living Inside the (Operating) System: Community in Virtual Reality (draft).* Available: http://jefferson.village.virginia.edu/pmc/Virtual.Community.html

Whitlock, Troy (ed.)
N.D. *MOO.Terrorism. Fuck Art, Let's Kill!: Towards a Post Modern Community. Terrorism in Cyberspace.* Available: ftp://jefferson.village.virginia.edu/pub/pubs/pmc/pmc-moo/MOO.Terrorism

Whorf, Benjamin Lee
1956 *Language, Thought and Reality. Selected Writings of Benjamin Lee Whorf.* Edited by John B. Carroll. Cambridge, Massachusetts: The MIT Press.

Young, Jeffrey R.
1994 *Textuality in Cyberspace. MUDs and Written Experience.* Available: http://ftp.game.org/pub/mud/text/research/textuality.txt